SAM MYERS

SAM MYERS
THE BLUES IS MY STORY

SAM MYERS AND JEFF HORTON

UNIVERSITY PRESS OF MISSISSIPPI / JACKSON

www.upress.state.ms.us

The University Press of Mississippi is a member of the
Association of American University Presses.

Photograph on page iii courtesy of Jeff Horton

First edition 2006

∞

Library of Congress Cataloging-in-Publication Data
Myers, Sam, 1936–
   Sam Myers : the blues is my story / Sam Myers and
Jeff Horton.— 1st ed.
     p. cm. — (American made music series)
   Includes discography (p. 145), song catalog (p. 155),
bibliographical references (p. 163), and index.
   ISBN-13: 978-1-57806-895-1 (cloth : alk. paper)
   ISBN-10: 1-57806-895-9 (cloth : alk. paper)
   ISBN-13: 978-1-57806-896-8 (pbk. : alk. paper)
   ISBN-10: 1-57806-896-7 (pbk. : alk. paper) 1. Myers,
Sam, 1936– —Biography. 2. African American musicians—
Biography. I. Horton, Jeff. II. Title. III. Series.
   ML410.M986A3 2006
   781.643092—dc22
                                                    2006002215

British Library Cataloging-in-Publication Data available

TO LITTLE MILTON CAMPBELL

1934–2005

AND

CELESTE MYERS

1912–2005

CONTENTS

ACKNOWLEDGMENTS

My first thanks go to my wife, Robin, who pushed me to write Sam Myers's life story. Her slashing red pen and brisk editorial comments went a long way towards turning a rambling manuscript into a real book. A number of friends provided significant help, contacts, and moral support. Jay Brakefield, a distinguished blues author in his own right, did the first edit of a very rough draft, gave me some valuable tips on writing and structure, and recommended that I send the manuscript to Craig Gill, editor in chief at the University Press of Mississippi. Craig thought well enough of it to pass it on to the distinguished Dr. David Evans, director of the ethnomusicology/regional studies doctoral program at the University of Memphis. Dr. Evans provided insightful advice in showing me how to tighten and rearrange what was still a rough manuscript. He was very encouraging and helpful to an amateur blues biographer, and for that I am deeply grateful.

Several musicians were instrumental in the development of this story. Anson Funderburgh contributed a number of anecdotes and important historical background. Brian "Hash Brown" Calway detailed the intricacies of Sam's harmonica technique. Craig Horton and Vasti Jackson contributed valuable insight into recording sessions they did with Sam back in the day. Blues legends B. B. King and Robert Lockwood, Jr., both graciously provided material for the introduction. And I gratefully give special thanks to blues chanteuse Robin Banks, who first introduced me to Sam Myers back in 2001.

Dallas blues impresario Chuck Nevitt suggested the title for this book. As soon as I heard it, I knew it was the one. Don Ottensman, blues programming director of KNON radio in Dallas, generously provided me with vintage photos of Sam and many words of encouragement.

Sam has a network of friends who have kept him going through good times and bad. Foremost is Joe Jonas, who has worn out a couple of cars taking Sam to doctors' appointments, picking up his fine suits from the cleaners, and carrying him to gigs all over town. The inner circle also includes Patti Coghill, Brenda Greer, Ravis Guthrie, Joanna Iz, and Jeff "Harp Man" Reed.

Last and most important, I thank Sam Myers for giving me, a mere fan who became a friend, the opportunity to learn about the blues in a direct and personal way that few have been privileged to experience. I am proud to tell his story, in his own words.

INTRODUCTION

The idea of writing Sam Myers's life story came to me because of
bowling. People who know Sam are aware that he is legally blind and
somewhat infirm due to diabetes and gout. But as it turns out, Sam
loves to go bowling with his friends. Somehow, he can see just enough,
in the right kind of way, to be able to bowl a pretty fair game. I've seen
him throw three strikes in a row.

One night in early 2002 I drove Sam to the local bowling alley
to meet up with our friends. On the way over, he told me a very
detailed and hilarious story about the time when he and Elmore James
ran a moonshine still on the banks of the Pearl River near Jackson,
Mississippi. I wished that I had a tape recorder with me and thought
that perhaps a retelling would make a good magazine article. My wife,
Robin, said that I needed to write a book about Sam's life instead.

Sam is very well known in the Dallas blues community, where he
turns up at regular jams when he's not on the road, and he has many
fans around the country and the world. His peers regard him with
affection and respect. They love to tell their favorite "Sam stories."

Among the artists he has known and worked with over the years
are B. B. King and Robert Lockwood, Jr., both of whom were kind
enough to share with me their thoughts on Sam.

"Well, I don't remember exactly when I met Sam Myers, it's been such a long time," King told me. "I think he's a great man, a great musician, and a wonderful storyteller. He's always been up-and-up with me and he's a nice person to be around. I think there's just one Sam Myers."

Lockwood said, "I've been knowing Sam for so long I can't think of how we met. I've been knowing him almost all of his life. We worked together off and on for near twenty years. He's a damn good musician, he's a nice person, and he's my friend, my best friend."

But even with friends like these and after fifty years in the business, Sam Myers never became a household name. There are many fabulously talented and hard-working bluesmen and blueswomen just like Sam, who've poured their music from their hearts all their lives in obscurity and never got the chance to have their stories told. This is my effort to rectify that situation with Sam.

—JEFF HORTON

SAM MYERS

CHAPTER 1

EARLY YEARS

Samuel Joseph Myers was born in Laurel, Mississippi, on February 19,
1936. He is the oldest child of Ollie and Celeste Myers. Until recently, both
resided in Jackson, Mississippi; Celeste passed away during the aftermath
of Hurricane Katrina in September 2005. Sam was followed by Mary Nell
and Wardell (both deceased) and Ollie, Jr., who now lives in Rose Hill,
Mississippi.

Located in Jones County in the southeast region of Mississippi known
as the Piney Woods, the city of Laurel was founded in 1882. At the turn
of the century, the railroads opened the region for large-scale timber
production, and the Eastman-Gardiner Company built the nation's first
large-scale lumber mill near Laurel. More mill companies soon followed
and made Laurel one of the largest mill towns in the South. Within a few
years, Laurel milled and shipped more yellow pine than anyplace else
in the world. In 1926, William Mason discovered a process for making
durable, inexpensive hardboard from the massive amounts of wood waste
produced by several mills owned by his wife's family in Laurel. This
material, dubbed Masonite, is still in use all over the world.

Because of the sandy soil and heavily forested terrain, pre–Civil War
Jones County (named for the Revolutionary War naval hero John Paul
Jones) depended far less on slave labor than the richer cotton country of

the Mississippi Delta a hundred miles to the northwest. A county census at the time tallied fewer than five hundred slaves and "free men of color." Partly as a result of less farming and sharecropping in that part of the state and the many relatively well-paying jobs in the railroads and lumber mills, Jones County escaped much of the misery brought about by the Civil War and Reconstruction. While life was still filled with hard work for most of the rural population, 1940s Laurel, Mississippi, was a good place for a visually impaired black child to grow up.

Sam contracted juvenile cataracts when he was seven years old. Two surgeries to restore his vision proved unsuccessful. Sam is not totally blind; he can make out shapes and shadows, and he can recognize familiar faces if they are close enough. He wears black-framed glasses with thick lenses and walks slowly and carefully to avoid obstacles. Possibly as a result of losing any workable sight at such a young age, Sam's memory and other senses are particularly acute. He was taught to read Braille, and for a while he used a Braille typewriter to write down lyrics to songs he composed. Now he mostly relies on a prodigious memory and a faithful stenographer, Joanna Iz, who publishes Southwest Blues magazine in Dallas, Texas. While Sam can read using Braille, he has never been able to write even his own name by hand, and he cannot read regular print. Sam uses a stamp to sign documents and autographs. The stamp's imprint was written in script by his close friend Joe Jonas. Sam will sign autographs by hand if coaxed, but the result is an illegible scrawl.

This chapter covers Sam's early life at home. Part of the narrative includes statements gathered from Sam's father, Ollie, his son Willie Earl, and his boyhood friend Eddie Booth during a 2002 visit by the author to Ollie's home, which was then in Mobile, Alabama. Sam's mother, Celeste, was living at the time in a nearby nursing home, the victim of a severe stroke some ten years before. Bedridden and unable to speak, she recognized Sam instantly when he came to see her, grasping for his hand as only

a mother will do. Sam's father visited her every day, but sadly, he also
suffered a stroke in early 2004. He lived in the same nursing home in
Jackson, Mississippi, as his wife until her recent passing.

I'm the oldest of four kids. I grew up in Laurel, Mississippi, with two
brothers and a sister. As a child I lived a very country life, and went off
to a separate school from my brothers and sister when I was about ten
years old. They attended public school, but I went away to school at
Piney Woods, south of Jackson on Highway 49. After school was out, I
would spend just a little time at home, like a week or two at the most.
Then I would go up to Chicago to visit family.

Back home my father was a sharecropper. He also worked road construction and in the timber industry with logs, pulpwood, and Masonite, that sort of stuff. Then he worked on the railroads. When I was at
home during the summer, my brothers and sister and I just played with
the kids in the neighborhood.

Ollie Myers (Sam's Father):
Sam's daddy and uncle were in the woods working one day. It was in
July, hot weather. Sam was about twelve years old. He was bringing them
their lunch when he got into a mess of yellow jackets. His uncle heard the
dishes falling and Sam hollering. His uncle said, "Oh, that boy done got
in that yellow jacket nest!" Sam was bringing a big lunch: sweet potatoes,
peas, greens, and tea in a jug to drink. He had a whole dishpan of food.
You could hear him singing as he was coming along, whistling and sing-
ing. We went up there and those sweet potatoes, peas, the jug of tea, it
was all over and full of yellow jackets. We had a time getting those yellow
jackets off of him!

At that time they would broadcast *The Game of the Day* every day of
the week on the Mutual Radio Network. I wanted to hurry back to the

house because the game would come on at one o'clock. It was about quarter to twelve when I left, and when I got to where they was working it was exactly twelve o'clock. They had told me about these yellow jackets. Their nest was in an old stump. I just didn't remember to go around it. I walked right up to it, and my foot bumped that son of a gun and all them yellow jackets come out of that durn thing and got on me and started crawling. When I went to take my hand to fight 'em off, about three of them bit me at once and then that food went everywhere, all over the woods.

Ollie:
Yes, sir, I can't remember the song he was singing, but he was whistling and singing as he was coming out of the woods, but it cut out when those yellow jackets got him!

My childhood was a unique thing; I used to be into a whole lot of stuff. We'd get a bunch of kids together, and we'd steal watermelons. Wherever we'd see a watermelon patch, we'd bust the watermelons open and get the heart out, if they were ripe, just nothing but the heart, and we'd eat it right there. There was a guy who had some great big ones in his field. There was a neighbor girl who nearly went blind behind that. This guy was sitting on his porch, he had just got through cleaning his rifle, and he had gone to sleep. There was a big wasps' nest on a fence pole at the corner of his house. Great big wasps' nest, those red ones, we called them "guinea wasps." Everybody made it through his fence except for this one girl. Some fool, I don't know who it was, shook the fence and knocked the nest off, and every one of those wasps got on that girl. She hollered, and we pulled her on through. That man jumped up to see what the noise was. He was nice about it. He said, "All y'all had to do was ask me and I would have given you all the watermelons you wanted." But see, back then, wasn't nothing good unless you were stealing it. Since it had happened on his property, he put the girl in the hospital, and he made sure she got whatever she needed. Her parents didn't press charges or nothing.

The wasps had stung her, and by that being done in summer, it was hot weather, she blanked out and lost consciousness. She was blind for a long time. That man thought that he was responsible for that happening. And he took care of her, all the medical stuff that she needed. Later on, her folks moved up into Laurel, Mississippi. When she was about eighteen or so they moved her upstairs in their house, and somehow she fell coming down the stairs, hit her head, and her sight came back. She was still a young woman, and she got back to where she could see again.

Eddie Booth (Sam's Childhood Friend):
Me and Sam used to walk down Highway 15, going to the dance. He would be walking along in front, and I'd be walking along behind him, and he'd be telling all those good jokes. And I'd be back there behind him laughing. He'd say, "Hey, Bubba, come on, we got to get on down there. Tighten it up." And I'd say, "You tighten up!" We'd get there and he'd say, "What you gonna do, Sonny?" I'd say, "I'm not gonna do nothing, I'm fixin' to dance!" Sam sure could dance too, yes, sir. Me and him had some times!

Me and Sam and Ollie Junior used to play baseball with a can. We'd go home in the evening time, our hands all cut up. So we finally got us a real ball, and we'd stay out there and play. Man, we was bad then, when we got that ball. We'd be throwing that ball around, playing like the pros. Yeah, we was tough then when we got us a real ball.

When I was about twelve, maybe thirteen, something happened as to why I smoke Camels today. My dad was working road construction, and we were staying in this big house that was up on pillars that held the house up off the ground. He would have cigarettes in little traveling cases. What we would do, we'd steal his cigarettes and put them under that little crawl space under the house. If we caught him not looking or if he was gone, we would go outside and get those cigarettes that we had hidden. That's where we would do our smoking, my brothers and me and my cousin. He used to come over and we all would hang together; he lived close, he was my mother's sister's son. We'd just be smoking and going on.

My dad took out so many packages at one time, we looked at it like he had so many he wouldn't miss the ones that we were getting. But what he did, he just decided not to pull out so many packages at once. He took maybe a couple of packs with him to work, and he left one or two lying around, just to see who was really smoking his cigarettes. So he came back and those cigarettes was open. He knew he didn't open them, because he had the ones he was going to smoke with him. He said, "Well, one of these days I'm going to find out definitely who's getting these cigarettes." There was a soap powder that was made back then called Gold Dust. What he did was to leave just three or four cigarettes out. He took the tobacco out of them, unbeknownst to us, and he put some of that Gold Dust in, and then he put the tobacco back in the end of it. And man, I was the first one to get one of 'em. And let me tell you, that was the worst thing that ever happened. I got dizzy, then I had a headache. I felt like somebody was walking around in my head with shoes with iron taps on the heel. I never tried that again! He said to me, "Well, now I've found out who's been getting my cigarettes. What I'm going to do, when you turn the age of fourteen, if you're going to continue to smoke, I'm going to buy you your first pack of cigarettes." And that's what he did.

I was able to eventually buy my own because they were about twenty cents a pack. I wouldn't buy nothing but Camels, and my brothers, they would always buy the loose ones, you could get two for a nickel. But I was pretty much like a hustler, you know, I just was ready to buy me a pack. My dad said once, "Well, I see you're still smoking. Give me a cigarette." I said, "I'm going to give you a pack." He said, "No, I don't want a whole pack, just give me one cigarette." I said, "No, I'm going to give you a whole pack. We're wearing the same shoe now. You bought my first pack, and if I could afford it, don't you think it'd be the right thing to do, to give you one?" He said, "I never heard you talk like that before." I said, "Well, if you want just one cigarette, just take it, and then if you don't want the pack, just say so. But there they're laying, over there by my case." He said, "Well, I do like that case." I said, "I got two of them, you take that one and the pack of cigarettes." So ever since then, whenever I'd run out he'd throw me a pack, and every time when he'd run out I'd throw him a pack.

I wasn't able to read and write like my brothers and sister. The type of education that I needed to learn, and things that I needed to know in life, they didn't teach it in public school. I wasn't able to see, because I had a juvenile cataract eye condition for quite a spell. I had an operation the same year I started to school, about age seven. They couldn't do a whole lot, but they didn't do what they could have done either. A Doctor Bell, he took the cataract off my eye, but he left parts of the roots still there. Later on, it grew back. When he took the cataract off the first time, I got back to where I could see pretty good. I could see better out of my left eye than I could my right, but I still had to wear glasses to support both eyes. I have a nerve condition, too, where my eyes dance a lot. Because of that, people have asked me, "Why not have surgery again?" I said, "Well, you know, I haven't really thought about it," but even now, I can see how to move about and go different places where people who have the same handicap don't. Sometimes I can see what's going on when people with perfect vision don't know what's happening. So I had my eyes operated on again when I was fourteen, in Memphis at the John Gaston Hospital.

It was the charity hospital back then. I tell a lot of people when I go to Memphis, "This is where my eyes were operated on, the first time I'd ever been to Memphis." It wasn't no big deal, it was just one of those things. Coming up from a poor background, I never let that stand out in front of me like a lot of people, accepting self-pity and stuff like that. I've never been that kind of way. From a child coming up, I learned one thing: if you want a strong something to happen to you in life, you gotta be strong.

I managed to survive a lot of times in places and in situations where it wouldn't help if people had their perfect vision. I've learned to survive better than a lot of them, and it don't look to me as if I'm as misfortunate as they are. I feel I am blessed and just as fortunate as a lot of people even when having a handicap. I look at it like self-pity is something that I don't need, and it's something that I don't stick out in front of me. I look at it like, hey, we're all human beings here, so what is fair for the next person is just as fair for me too. A lot of people look at it a little different, but it's a true thing.

Ollie:

Sam's mama, Celeste, loved to go fishing, but she never would carry Sam to fish because he couldn't see to get along in the woods. Celeste and me would go hunting with Corrine Tatum, that's another one of her lady friends, and Ashton Jones and his wife. We'd have those blue jeans that were fleece-lined, rubber boots, and Celeste had her flashlight and a little old dog. Old Spot was his name. He didn't bark when he was running a coon, so she had to hang a bell on his neck. She'd hear that bell rattling when he was running. When he got a coon up a tree, then he'd bark.

They used to go fishing on Friday nights, just like people be going out on weekends nowadays. They'd take their pans and grease and coffeepot and they'd cook the fish right on the creek bank.

Ollie:

*I had fourteen head of hound dog that I used to go hunting with. I had a
.22 rifle I shot coon with, and I had an old double-barreled shotgun that
I deer-hunted with. It had two hammers on it. I had buckshot in one
barrel and a slug in the other. And all those dogs, I didn't buy no dog food.
Celeste would cook potatoes and bread, cook up a bunch of stuff like that
for those dogs. Some of 'em I had tied up, some of 'em I didn't. I had a
trough out where I'd feed 'em. Now that was her special dog, that little old
Spot. We'd go coon hunting and those hound dogs couldn't find nothing.
But you could hear that bell rattling, "Ting-a-ling, ting-a-ling!" And you
know he done struck a track then. Them other dogs, when they'd hear
that bell rattling like that, they'd take off, too. And he didn't bark until he
treed up what he was running.*

He was a smart dog, too. We had another dog; he was one of them
redbone hounds. Dan was his name. We had another one named
Flora. That one hung herself.

Ollie:

*She was in heat, you know. I had her shut up in a crib so the dogs couldn't
get to her, and I didn't have the door fastened up enough. She crawled out,
and the chain, when she fell out, she just hung up there. I got up the next
morning and there she was, hanging out, done choked herself to death.*

*When we was fishing, we'd take a big can and get some water. To
catch them catfish, we'd set out hooks, find us a good long place and set
out fifteen, twenty big, long hooks. Get us some grub worms out of an
old rotten log, put 'em on them hooks. We'd fish in the daytime when the
creeks would be up, catch us some fish, cook 'em, and when night come,
we'd make some coffee. We'd be sitting out there cleaning them fish. We'd
have a meal and we'd be down there all night long cooking fish, catching
them yellow cats. Cook 'em as we catch 'em.*

Me and another boy that was raised up with Sam, White was his name, me and him and Ashton Jones, one night we caught a hundred yellow cat. A hundred of them, and there was some big fresh-water eels. They a fresh-water fish, wasn't no salt-water fish. And we caught a blue cat with a forked tail. We caught a hundred of them yellow cats, I never will forget it. And seven of them eels, big old blue eels, 'bout that long. I know it was seven eels. I don't think but one of them was a blue cat. We had a whole load of fish coming out of there that Sunday morning.

Sam never did go fishing or hunting with us. He couldn't see how to get around much in the woods at night. But he'd sure enough go to them clubs. We called 'em shops, they was in the country. We called 'em road-houses in the city. Back then, you could play a record for a nickel. They'd stay up all night long, playin' and a-dancin', whoopin' and hollerin', singin' and showin' out.

Author:
What has it meant for you to have Sam turn out to be such a famous and respected blues musician?

Ollie:
I'm glad he's had fun. I'm sure enough wonderful proud that he's got people, his friends, seeing out after him like they do. There are things he's done for himself that I wouldn't have been able to do for him.

Willie Earl (Sam's son):
I'm proud that he's got as far as he has with whatever he's been trying to do with his life in music. I know he's got to like it, because he's been doing it all these years, and he's seen his ups and downs in it. I'm just glad that he's made it far as he has, to really see some success out of it. And I'm glad I have his inspiration, having the background of somebody in my life like him, to say that I have some influence in music and a father like him

who has kept going through the things that he's had with his life. He kept on. I hope he has great success in whatever he does from here on out. I'm glad he ran into some people that really help him, that keep him going in the right direction. He done seen a lot of hard times in music, and the time when he got started, he probably wasn't getting anything out of it back then. I'm just happy that it's paying off for him now. I wish him more of the best of luck. I'm very proud of him.

CHAPTER 2

COTTON FIELDS, RAILROADS, AND SAWMILLS

While conditions in pre–World War II Jones County, Mississippi, were marginally better for much of the rural black population than in other places in the region, life for many of Sam's contemporaries was nevertheless filled with long, hard work. Compared to the number of workers in the more agricultural areas of the state, fewer people toiled in the fields surrounding Sam's hometown of Laurel. But the tradeoff for the somewhat better pay and working conditions in the mills and on the railroads was frequently injury and sometimes death.

It wasn't always fun then, but after I grew up I thought about it many times, being on the farm and seeing how people pick cotton. I even picked a few bolls myself. One thing that was real interesting was when I was a water boy during cotton-picking season. I had this big water carrier filled with cold water. People wouldn't eat much during the hot weather. The sun would be beating down, and a lot of them would have umbrellas to keep their heads shaded. I would be walking along and they would holler, "Water boy!" I had some cups on a big rod, so if someone wanted some water, I would take this cup and pour the water for them. Some of them would have their own special drinking cup, and I wouldn't have to give them a cup every time. I would just fill theirs up. Some would say, "I want a rock in the bucket." That meant a hard piece of ice.

On the second day I was doing this, I wasn't feeling good. With me getting tired, I could imagine how tired they would be. But that was their only means of work at that time, to make what little money they could picking cotton. The only thing they were interested in was getting their sacks filled. They would run eleven-foot cotton sacks, to ones even longer, maybe sixteen-foot, and they would fill those sacks up. The first thing I thought of when I saw them was they was just making horses out of themselves. Things can come to mind like that. I said, "No, I don't think I want to do this," so I went and carried the water. What would happen, by the time you thought you got it made, finished with all that water, someone was always hollerin' way across the field, "Water boy! Water boy!" It was a big bucket with a dipper in it, and if I were to empty it I would have to walk way back up to the shed where they weighed the cotton and fill it up again and do the same thing over.

They would start picking cotton at sunup because it would be cooler. They could get more in that way, and by the time the sun rose up to about twelve o'clock high, they would have picked a long ways in the field. So I got going when they started in the morning, I'd say about eight o'clock, and by twelve o'clock, I was worn out. They would take a break for lunch, and then a lot of them would be interested in getting back to the fields, trying to pick enough cotton to earn enough money to make it. A lot of families would, I'd estimate, pick maybe three hundred pounds apiece. There would be men, women, even little kids, maybe ten or twelve years old, who were out of school. They could pick only so much, so they'd have a littler sack, picking along-side their parents. They would take their little amount and pour it into a bigger sack. And they also got paid for what they did. But a lot of times, the sun would be so hot they wouldn't let the kids come out.

The first picking would be right about August, and sometimes they'd pick cotton way into October, but normally it'd be real heavy in the months of August and September. After October, it'd be what they call scrapping cotton. I used to stand and watch them and I'd say, "These people must sure be tired doing this." But even back then music was in my head. I remember one day I went and made a couple of rounds on the water wagon. I went like I was going to get some more water to bring back to the field. I set that bucket and cup rack down, and that's when I left and went to Chicago. That was the last time I was in the fields. I used to go back home on school break and see them working like that in those fields, and I thought that was really a terrible way to make a living.

When I was thirteen or fourteen, I would go to Chicago during the summer. That would be during the time before cotton-picking season would start, and I would come back a couple of weeks before school, right in the middle of picking season. To me that was a really brutal way to make it. The farmers back then, after they picked so much cotton, it was just like the plantation owners in the Delta. We didn't live in the Delta, but those rows in the fields, they seemed to be just as long as the rows in a Mississippi Delta field. And it was just so hot back then. When they would take the cotton to the gin, I used to go down there a lot of times, just to see those big pipes and things. Some of them would have a wagon, some of them had tractors pulling the wagon, and some of them would have trailer trucks that was hauling. At the gin they'd drop that pipe on the wagon, where the cotton was loosely set, and it would suction it right up into the gin. They'd have the seeds going one way and the cotton going another. The cotton would go into this big thing called a hopper and they'd weigh it. They'd weigh it twice, and when it got up to fourteen hundred pounds it would be one bale. Then they'd put a metal band around it to lock it all together, and then they would jam it over. They would write the person's name on it, whose farm it was. They'd get all this cotton weighed and when they'd settle up with you, the guy would always say, "Well, you made about fourteen bales, you know, about fourteen bales of cotton was your part." But actually you made more than that. They'd say, "You like to came out." That meant you almost picked as much as you were supposed to have picked, to pay back all the money that you had borrowed from the farm store.

That was their slogan, "You just about made it, but try harder next year." They'd be cheating you all the time; if you picked sixteen or eighteen bales, they'd say you made fourteen. There wouldn't be no complainin', though. They'd send these samples back to the farmer who owned the farm. The farmer would say, "Well, you know, you like to came out. For Christmas, you're going to need some extra money." And he'd loan you three or four hundred dollars, and if you had a big family and everybody needed a pair of shoes, that wasn't going to do you no good. You'd get credit at the company store, but you could never work it off.

To help pass the time, they would be singing in the fields. They'd sing these different songs, strung out all over the field. Sometimes they'd be singing the same song; other times it would be different songs. I never will forget, they would be just making up stuff to sing, like about the rain. Like, "I'm not gonna work another day without pay, and it seems like it's not gonna rain no more," because you knew when it rained, regardless of how much cotton was in the field, you couldn't pick it because you had water in the rows. That is how a lot of blues songs was written.

It was rough back then in the area where I lived, but it wasn't as rough as it was in the Mississippi Delta. By Laurel being a city, it was a little bit better. They didn't have as much cotton and stuff around

Laurel and Jackson. That's where your cotton would come to. They would have a gin, and they would have oil mills where they made cottonseed oil. And you know, people didn't get paid much for a lot of the work they did back then, but they had better facilities then than they do today. You take today's railroads, it was the same way. When my dad worked on the railroad, they had to do manual labor in putting those rails down. I used to watch them doing that. It'd be ten men on a rail, four on each side and one on each end. These men would get under the rail, and they'd pick it up off the flatcar. That iron is heavy, and they would be standing there holding that rail up. They would pull the flatcar out from under, and they'd drop that thing onto the crossties. Then the other guys who were standing there came along with mauls and drove spikes in it. One guy would drop the plate down, the plate that goes at the end of the tie, and then they'd put the spike into that. The spikes were set to the tie, and then they'd get it all lined up and everything.

Most railroads have white gravel; they'd take that gravel and put it between the ties. That was really hard work, but they had better railroads back then. The cotton fields and railroads went hand in hand. You were a laborer regardless, and the only difference between the railroad and being a sharecropper picking cotton was the railroad was a year-round, lifetime job. If you were a farmer, you were still just as important as the next man, but you didn't get paid. The railroad had better pay than a lot of the jobs, because railroad has been federal for a long time. Then, every year they had more fringe benefits. They had a great thing going.

I don't remember what year it was when they started discontinuing a lot of passenger trains; then the federal government took it over. They started doing a lot of railroad work by machine, and the railroads and the maintenance of them wasn't as good as it was when the guys did it by hand from the real labor days. And you would all the time hear tell of trains having a wreck or running into something, but when a train had an accident back then in the early days, it was at a crossing or something like that. Nowadays, they have accidents with trains when they're just riding right along, and there are plenty more accidents now than there were back then, due to the fact that a machine is doing the work a man used to do. Nowadays one man can operate a machine to put down the spikes and stuff; they do it with a machine that took six men out of work. Just one machine. And the work that the machine does, it just isn't as good as the work that man-power did back in the days of the steam engine.

I still have a strong infatuation with trains. When I was going to school, my mother would come out to Piney Woods and we'd go back home on the train. I loved that. On one of those trips she told me, "Son, now you're a big boy. I'm going to ask you something, but you got to promise me that you won't get scared." So I said, "What's that?" She said, "Suppose you come home on the train by yourself?" I said, "I would love that!" That was my first experience, and after that I would go everywhere by myself, and ever since I always had this thing for trains. I haven't done it since I've been living here in Dallas, but I used to go out and stand by the railroad and watch the passenger trains go by.

There was a friend of mine, an older man named Sid Edwards, who worked driving one of those big trucks that hauled bulldozers and road graders. He was working with a construction company out of Memphis, but he'd come home to Jackson every weekend. Sometimes he would go to some parts of Louisiana to deliver on Sunday evening so it all could be together, ready for them to start work Monday morning. I said, "Man, you've got a lot of gears and shifts in there." He said, "Yeah, this is what is called a twin-stick. It has thirteen forward gears and another with a split shift." He told me that when he started changing gears, he'd get up to five, and when he'd kick in that "Road Ranger" he could get up to speed.

Not far from where we lived they had a gravel pit, and Sid used to drive what was called a "dirt train." Sid worked in this gravel pit where they shifted sand and gravel out onto the trains to go to different areas. He would drive the train, switch the cars in to be loaded, and then he would bring them up to the main line for the locomotives to pick them up and transfer them to where they needed to be. He taught me a lot about driving a train. A lot of people look at it as being hard, but it's a real simple thing. All of it works by levers. Once you get it started, you have a lever that you push to a certain mark, and that picks up the speed to how fast you want to go. I learnt from that, and when he had some time off I followed him near everywhere he went. When I'd be home from Piney Woods, my mother would fix me a sack lunch just like I would be going off to work. Sid would pick me up in the morning, and I would just follow him around all day. Ordinarily I wouldn't be allowed to be on the job with him, but he got it straight with his supervisor that he would take care of me and see that nothing happened.

Being around Sid got me even more interested in music. I used to love the way he whistled. He was about one of the best whistlers I ever heard. He could whistle most any song, like "The Tennessee Waltz" or "Blue Moon of Kentucky," and he would whistle a lot of blues songs. He could even whistle the sound of a bird. All through the day when I'd be around with him, he'd be doing his work and then he'd whistle tunes for me. He loved teacakes, so when we would stop by the house, Mama would fix him teacakes with ginger and cinnamon in them. Mama would ask him, "Sid, do you have your lunch?" and she'd fix him a big paper bag of those teacakes. He kept a big jug of water up in the cab of that engine, and that's all he would do, eat those cakes and drink that water. He would make the day like that.

If I didn't see him right away in the morning I would really be out of focus. Sometimes he'd be late coming by, and I'd wonder where he was. We'd go on, and he would show me different things about the train. When he would get all of his loads ready, it wouldn't take him long, because he had a big steam shovel on the end of the loader that they had on the train. He'd take a couple of scoops and fill up a truck or a boxcar. He showed me how to start it and where the gearshifts were, and I learnt from there how to crank up all that stuff. His thing was, when he was going to show you how to do something, the first thing he would do was to show you how to start and stop it in case you were going to run into something, or if you weren't going in the right direction. He would show you what lever would keep it level and on a straight path. All that grew up in me, and I learnt pretty good after that.

With Sid and another guy who worked at a sawmill, we never did have to worry about toys and food at Christmas time. Them and my dad was real good friends, and they would get fruit and toys for us. That was a happy time for me. But it's strange how things can happen. I had been home from school for two days in the summertime. One morning, instead of coming by the house, Sid was running pretty late so he went straight on to work. Something just didn't let him come by to get me on that particular day. After a while we heard a big explosion. A boiler had blown up on the train he was driving, and he was killed. If he had picked me up on that day, I would have been right there with him. Boy, that was a great loss. I think about that old man, as long as it's been, I think about him right today.

There's something else I never will forget. Ben Maxwell, he was a sawmill guy. He could fix anything or do any kind of work around a sawmill that needed to be done. He lit the boiler, he worked in the saw shop sharpening saws, but his main job was running the head saw. When a log was cut into lumber, he had those saws where he sat on a stool and he took a piece of lumber and put it over on one side for two-by-fours. On the other side he may be cutting two-by-sixes or whatever. And then he ran a cut-off saw. All the saws were around him on that big stool. When the lumber came off the logs, they came out of a big house where they have big, giant saws. When the logs come through the door, they just rip 'em open with the rip saws and then the other saws took over.

One day, Ben got his leg cut off. Wasn't noticing what he was doing, and it would be so noisy in that mill they had to use shortwave radios. Somebody would be on the conveyor belt when the lumber was coming off it, and if they weren't watching what was going on, he would holler, "One coming!" Then they would know to move back and get ready to mark it. They would cut the ends of 'em off, put 'em on another conveyor belt, and then they'd go out and stack 'em. A guy would come through with a forklift and they'd take 'em and stack 'em in the yard until they had a big pile of 'em. And that mill didn't throw away nothing. The sawdust went into a big vat that looked like a boxcar. They had some kind of chemical that had big pipes blowing it into the vat where the sawdust was. It would turn that sawdust red and it would be just like a powder, so they would make floor sweeper out of it. The only thing that they wouldn't save would be the bark of a tree.

So this guy Ben Maxwell was cutting some boards one day and wasn't noticing what he was doing. As long as he'd been working there, one of those saws just cut his leg off. He reached down and pulled it up onto that durn conveyor belt. He hollered to them, "If you see anything red, that's part of me!" Cut his durn leg off as smooth as my hand, just above his boot top. The guys rushed to him and said they were going to take him to the doctor. Ben said, "No, I've got to work." They said, "But man, your leg is cut off!" He said, "Damn, it wasn't no good no way, wasn't nothing but a botheration." They knew he was in hysterics, and they grabbed him up off of that stool, and he was fighting them off. They knew then that there was really something wrong with him. The accident wasn't the cause of his death, but he died a few years later when he got to where he couldn't do anything more with just one leg. It must've been that it just worried him to death.

CHAPTER 3

PINEY WOODS

In 1909 educator Dr. Laurence C. Jones founded the Piney Woods School in rural Rankin County, Mississippi, a few miles south of Jackson. He began the school with a handful of children and held his first classes in an old split-log sheep shed. The shed remains preserved on the campus as a historical exhibit and still contains the ancient piano that was used to teach music. Today the nationally recognized school occupies over two thousand wooded acres that includes a five-hundred-acre working farm and a campus of classroom buildings, dormitories, and activity centers. Piney Woods graduates small classes of about twenty students every year, and almost all of them move on to college or careers in the military. The school has an outstanding reputation for academics and has been featured twice on the CBS news program 60 Minutes. When Sam began his schooling there in 1947, Piney Woods was also home to the state school for the blind.

Piney Woods was not like any ordinary school; it was more like a trade school. Some people looked at Piney Woods as being a correctional facility or a prison, but it wasn't. It was a school of higher learning, in a country life. Whatever trade you wanted to learn, you could decide on what you wanted to be in life, like a brick mason, a carpenter, a cement finisher, or a musician. If you wanted to be a doctor, they even had a hospital where you could learn that. They had any type of work that you wanted to do right there. They had to travel off the campus for only a few things. The buildings were built by the hands of the staff and the students. They grew a lot of their own food and had cows for milk. The students learned how to help pick the food crops and how to help tend the cows. That was part of their trade and their learning as they grew up. Of course I was interested in music, and that is what I mostly studied from age ten up to where I am now. It was music that was the cause of me knowing what two and two is. Even today, I look back on my life and the early years and see where music has played a very important part.

One thing that was interesting about the school was that we never had any performers to come on campus to do our social activities. The band was large enough so that we played our own social functions and gatherings. Sometimes in the summer we would sign up everyone to do it. We would travel across the country with the Piney Woods Band Glee Club. That's where I learned a lot about singing, doing a lot of gospel music and such. Back in the forties it would get super cold indoors compared to what it is now with modern heat, so we would sing gospel music in the dormitory. What I remember is that we had only steam from the radiators to keep us warm. We would get in a group in a room and do a lot of this singing just to keep from freezing.

Ollie Myers:
When he was going to school at Piney Woods, Sam's mother, Celeste, left to go out to visit him when the buses were about to go on strike. She had sold a calf and bought a Smith & Wesson .38, I never will forget that. She was on the bus, looking in her bag for something, and she had her flashlight on the side. The bus driver told her he couldn't stop at Piney Woods, because the strike was going to start in Jackson at midnight, and

it was quarter to twelve then. She said, "Right here is where I'm going."
He said, "Yes, I know where Piney Woods is, but I'm not supposed to
stop." And she said that when she was looking through her bag, the driver
spotted her pistol and flashlight. He said, "Well now, you know letting
you off here will be at your own risk, but I think you're able to take care
of yourself!"

Unlike some of the kids at Piney Woods who got into mischief and
stuff, I was sort of a quiet kid. I really didn't want to go to the school,
and I tried several times to run away. I didn't know any better. As a
matter of fact, I didn't even know where to go. I just didn't want to be
where I was. They put a gentleman with me, a Mr. Jonas Brown. We all
called him "J. B." He was there to find out what I really liked or what I
didn't like about the school. He would ask from time to time how I
was doing. I didn't think about it until later, after I found out what
I really liked about Piney Woods. We were standing out in front of
the dormitory one day, just talking. I guess I was about ten years old.
I always wanted somebody to read to me, so he was getting ready to
read to me, and I heard the band rehearsing, getting ready for a football game. I heard this sound that really struck my attention. I asked,
"What's that?" J. B. said, "Do you like it?" I said, "Yes, indeed! I like to
hear those horns." He said, "That's the band playing, getting ready for
the game." I asked, "Would they say anything if I went up there? I'd
like to go and listen to it." He said, "No, you can go anywhere on the
campus that you want to. Do you want to go?" I said, "I sure would."
So we went up there and walked in when they were getting ready to
take a break.

There was this young student named Anna Mae Williams who
blew trumpet. I never will forget, after J. B. introduced me to Mr.
Charles McGilvery, the band director, I went over to her and sat down.
I said, "What is that?" She told me, "A trumpet." I asked, "Can I see it?"

She said, "Sure. Do you want to learn to blow this one?" I said, "I'd like to, but right now I just want to listen." She told me then, "You can't sit here and listen and not take part in it." J. B. said, "It looks like you done found a friend." They started to play a march called "The Stars and Stripes Forever," and I said, "Boy, oh boy, I wonder could I be able to do that someday?" She said, "Yes, but you'll have to practice." I did have sense enough to know that. I said, "I'm not going to bother you all; I just love to listen." Mr. McGilvery told me I could stay as long as I wanted. Between songs Anna Mae would show me her horn and let me hold it. I said, "I sure would like to be able to blow like you're blowing, one day."

I never will forget, she said, "If you come tomorrow, I'll let you play this horn. It's a school horn; I'll bring my own horn and we'll blow along together. But you can't blow too loud because you don't know the song." I went back to the dormitory, and that stayed in my head the whole time. I couldn't wait until the next day came. Jonas Brown told the headmaster, "Well, music is what he likes. He likes the band." J. B. came to me that night and said, "What you've got to do, if you want to play in the band, you've got to learn something else to go along with that. So whatever they tell you to do about your books and your lessons, you've got to do it. Then you'll be all right." I said, "I will. I'll do that." He said, "It's not enough just to play in the band, you've got to learn your other lessons and let it stay with you." I started getting my lessons real good after that. This was a test to see what I really enjoyed in school, and it was the music. But I had to get my other things together before I could really do what I wanted to do.

Anna Mae brought the horn the next day and do you know, instead of just learning, I found that it was a gift that I had, to be in music. She showed me how to focus my lips on the mouthpiece; she showed me how to make the different keys and notes and how to shape my fingers. They started playing a song called "White Heat."

I messed up that one. The next one was called "Symphony C." It had a big-band sound and I almost got that one. Mr. McGilvery said, "Well, what are we going to do next?" I hollered out, "'The Stars and Stripes Forever'!" and I thought to myself, "Oh, my goodness, I messed up." They all looked and said, "Oh yeah, we can do that." They thought I was just saying something, that I was just going to listen. Then, somehow, when they started, "Da-da-da, da-da-da, da-da-da," I was playing that on the trumpet, and they all tricked me. Everybody looked right at me, but they started playing quiet. I was being heard by all of them, and after I played that part down, they all came up with a big, strong rhythm and played their parts, and then they started laughing. I said to myself, "Oh, they're laughing at me." Mr. McGilvery walked over to me and tapped me on the shoulder and said, "My dear boy, you did good." And from then on I got in the swing with the rest of them. And I thank that girl, Anna Mae Williams, wherever she is, right today, for me to be able to do that. She was a real good friend. That part of my schooling was where I really learnt the scales of music, listening to it by ear since I couldn't read the notes on the sheet music.

We used to hear a lot of radio there at the school. Jonas Brown had a radio that we would listen to. Jackson had one radio station we would listen to in the evenings. It was called WJDX. They had a show called *In the Groove*. Woodie Assaf used to broadcast that show every Monday, Wednesday, and Friday at 5:15. And then they had another one that would come on Tuesdays and Thursdays called *Jive Parade*, done by a guy called Alan B. Keaton. We would listen to this on J. B.'s radio just before we went to supper in the evenings. We couldn't wait to hear all these old standards. Jonas Brown would take another student, Andrew Oliver, and me to Jackson to buy records. They had a big record store on Farish Street called Hardwell and Cook's. We would go and get records for twenty-five cents back then, 45s and 78s. They didn't have the 33⅓s, the long-play albums, yet.

We would get a lot of those records and come back and listen to them, even during the daytime between our classes. I was blowing trumpet pretty good by then, I thought, and I went and got a harmonica, one of the plastic ones. I would listen to some of the music by John Lee Williamson, who was the original Sonny Boy Williamson. And the Big Three Trio, Calvin Boze, T-Bone Walker, Louis Jordan, all that music, we'd listen to it. I would take a harmonica, and with what I already knew about music at the time, I would try to find the key that that song was in. I'd find a harp with that key, and I would try to blow along with the songs. It took a long time. I'd collected a lot of them, because I would just go and buy a bunch of them and try to find a key for a particular song. So that worked for a while, and that's how I happen to blow the harmonica today.

Piney Woods was just like it says, Piney Woods Country Life School. You didn't have to be a special ed person to attend there. Some people looked at it as being like a prison, and I heard a lot of parents tell their kids, "All right, if you keep doing this or that, I'm going to send you to Piney Woods." Well, that's disgusting. It wasn't like that at all. Piney Woods was a school of higher learning. The reason I say that was because during those times a lot of public schools had their trials and tribulations and kids were going to school and really not learning nothing, just like today's kids.

At the time when I started, Piney Woods was also a place that housed people who were blind. They didn't get no state funding or nothing. The gentleman who founded the school, Dr. Laurence C. Jones, he would go and make speeches for Piney Woods projects. That's what they were supported on. It was more like a boarding school instead of a state school. And where I fit in, being visually impaired, that's what was happening at Piney Woods before the state took over the school for the blind. Now they have the workshops at the Mississippi Industries for the Blind in Jackson for the people who are visually impaired. Back during that time a lot of handicapped people would be on the streets shaking a cup as I would call it, what panhandlers do today. I get pretty angry when I see people do that.

Piney Woods always has been integrated. You had white, you had the Jewish, you had gentiles, you had Mexicans. In Piney Woods, they had everybody. It wasn't a white and black thing, and it wasn't a Mexican and a Jewish thing. Everybody was declared as one. But here's what a lot of people put a blanket over Piney Woods about. You went there to school, you did your studies, and the boys didn't mingle with the girls like a lot of schools let do. The girls had their social gatherings, and the boys had theirs. They had what were called matrons who did their job as they were supposed to have done, and it's the only school that I know of where there wasn't any babies born like you have in a lot of schools today. You pick up your paper or you turn on your TV and watch your six o'clock news, and you see where some girl at a school, it sounds sick, but she had a little boy or girl and stuffed it in the trashcan. You didn't see that there at Piney Woods. My mother's cousin, Ella Pearl Gant, was a matron of girls at Piney Woods for many years. She's buried right there at the school's cemetery, over by where Dr. Jones and his wife are buried.

They had a few teachers who said, "I'm doing this just because it's a job." But it was tough to find a job back then, and you had more people of differing nationalities to compete with. If you are a graduate of Piney Woods and you had it in your résumé or if you just mentioned the name "Piney Woods," you got a job. It was a school of higher learning that was recognized in music, like the schools of music at Berklee and Juilliard and North Texas State and the American Conservatory in Chicago. When you went to hear the commencement exercise, you would see the girls in their blue skirts and white blouses and the guys in their khaki suits with black ties and shined shoes, like the military. The athletic director, he had been in the military; his name was Lieutenant Colonel Payne.

All the kids, they loved him because he wasn't one of those instructors who was there just because it was a job. He would play and have fun with the kids. He'd be thinking about stuff he did in the military. He may call the guys out about four o'clock in the afternoon, between classes and dinner, and have them marching, or he might have all 250 boys lined up in front of the dormitory, counting, saying the numbers, like "One," and the next guy, "Two," and then "Three," and the next guy "Four," on like that, sounding off. He'd walk up and one might be standing there like he didn't want to be bothered, and he'd say to him, "What're you doing, looking all sour for?" He may grab him and whirl him around the shoulders and kick him in his behind, and they'd do the same thing to him. They'd all jump and grab him and do the same thing. He was happy most when they'd do that. Like a guy'd be standing up, talking to a girl, and he'd walk up and, he ate ice cream all the time, he'd have an ice cream cone in his hand, and he'd walk up and just stand there and say, "You wonder why I'm standing here? Well, you know, trouble me." And then they'd all just grab him, take their belts and whip him, and just kick him.

And do you know, that Mister Tough Guy, the kids knew what he was about. He was crazy about the kids. He'd always be playing and going on with them, and then, they knew when he meant business as an instructor. He boxed and wrestled with the kids, and some of them was just as good as he was at that sort of thing. That was just his lifestyle. I don't know whether he's living now or not. Last I heard, he had married a girl from Kosciusko named Anna Bee Foster, and they moved to Memphis. They had separated and he was operating a shoe-shine stand in Memphis, the last I heard.

Colonel Payne showed us how to go through a belt line. The way he had it set up, he had about eight or ten guys, standing and have belts, and they send you through the belt line, but if a man hit you more than once, they pulled his behind out of the line, and they'd have fifteen guys to give him a belt lashing. Boy, he was a tough guy. And that's why, when I went to Chicago, besides music, that's what gave me the idea of taking defense training for myself. I used to work out at the Joe Louis Gym, doing all this judo and all these different fancy handholds and stuff. Not that I've ever had to use it in any kind of way, but it's better to know it and not need it than to need it and not have it.

I had a bunch of sweethearts when I was coming up at Piney Woods. Even though music was my main thing at Piney Woods, I was playing football, trying to prove to a girl that I was a hero. She wound up marrying some guy that was studying to be a cement mason. I did all right through practice, then when we got out on the field for the first game, I like to got my neck broke. When the guy tackled me, they fell down on my behind. I was a running back. Boy, oh, boy, I was supposed to be pretty fast, but I was slow that day.

During the summer some of the band would travel all across the country as an all-girls orchestra, as part of their education. I was the only guy in the group, there to help out with things. We were traveling to Washington State, and while we were in Oregon, there was a guy who shot at a deer. It was up in the mountains, and just as he cracked that rifle, the bus went by. The girls was getting ready for bed, and he shot this girl, Willie Christine Jackson. Shot her in the leg. That man had a Jeep. That's the way they hunt out in Oregon, they have those Jeeps in the woods. I was sitting up in the cab with the driver, George Bishop. It was one of those big rigs, pulling a trailer bus, and them girls was crying, hollering, and going on, and that man know he had shot somebody, but he didn't know who it was. He must have known that mountain road, because he came by us, and when we got down the mountain he was there waiting, he had blockaded the road with his Jeep.

The first thing he did, he opened up the trailer wanting to know who it was that he shot. And the girl who got shot kept trying to get ready for bed, she didn't even know she was shot herself, and boy, that was a sad time for all of us. He told us he was going to contact her parents and let them know who he was and said whatever it would cost, he would take care of her hospital and medical bills. He told us what hospital to take her to, and better yet, he would lead us there. And boy, the girls was crying and going on and wondering was she going to live. But she just got shot in the leg. The bullet didn't stop and went all the way through. It would have broke her bones if it had lodged, but it was the soft part of the flesh where it went in. After we got to the hospital he said, "I want her to be able to walk just as good or better than she did before this happened." Whatever she wanted while she was in the hospital, she didn't have nothing to worry about.

He was some kind of owner of a chemical company or maybe a mill that did redwood and timber. He must have been a wealthy man, because he paid for every day that she was in the hospital. He always stayed in touch and made sure that the girls who was traveling with us and the bus driver knew how she was doing. And when we saw her again, it was about two weeks after school was set back in. She came back to school and everybody was glad to see her. She was telling us all how she missed us. Could you imagine, if you were a little person, about a hundred pounds and all these people were hugging you and going on, so glad to see you? I said, "Well, heck, this is the first time y'all have ever been this close together when you wasn't on stage." Boy, they ruled me out then!

My first great love was Anna Mae Williams. She was my dear sweetheart. She was older than me, but I had a crush on her then, and when we could get the drop on the teacher, we would be together like a hot date. Her parents lived in Jackson and she finished Piney Woods and started working at the Smith Robertson School in Jackson. Now it's a museum for a lot of historic people, but back then it was the first school for black students in Jackson. After I had been to Chicago and all around there and overseas I came back to Jackson. I used to live on Davis Street and she was up the street from me. And boy, when I heard she had gotten married and moved to Gary, Indiana, I said, "Now what can you say? She should have been my wife." But, heck, I wasn't into getting married or nothing like that then. But I had a crush on her from day one. I haven't heard from her now in quite a while.

But she had taught me something. If it hadn't been for her, I never would have been a trumpet player. In 2002 we played the Medgar Evers Homecoming for Charles Evers down in Mississippi, and I looked high and low for that girl. I hadn't seen her in about forty-five years or longer. I liked her because she was real tall and pretty. But I wound up being a bachelor, and I've been one ever since. Course, I've had my share of shacking up with women, though. That was just the way it was for me.

CHAPTER 4

GOING TO CHICAGO

The lure of playing music soon called to Sam from the big city of Chicago, as it had called to so many black musicians from Mississippi. But by 1951, when Sam was ready to move north to attend the American Conservatory of Music in Chicago, the scene had changed, and new opportunities abounded for the postwar generation of southern blacks. Unlike his elder relatives, Sam wasn't looking for work to escape from the plantations and mills of the Deep South. Instead he planned to further his music education in two ways: by studying in the classroom and by going to school in the clubs and on the rough streets of the South Side.

Sam learned his chops from watching legends of Maxwell Street like Buddy Guy, Howlin' Wolf, Muddy Waters, Little Walter, Wayne Bennett, and a man who remains to this day a great friend of Sam's, Robert Lockwood, Jr. Sam soon matured to the point where he was sitting in with local bands. And then in 1952, he met a man who would loom large in his life for the next ten years. That man was Elmore James.

When I left Mississippi for Chicago I was about fifteen. I had finished my studies at Piney Woods and considered myself to be one of the blessed in my time and area, to have received a scholarship to attend the American Conservatory of Music in Chicago. That's where I met a lot of the musicians who are heroic to a lot of the newcomers of today.

I lived with a cousin of mine first off, but you know how youngsters are, you want to get out and be making your own money and get your own place, and that's what I did. I was a music major, so while I attended school there, I went through a lot of instruments that I had dealt with at Piney Woods. For me, it was just a brush-up on them. I played piano and trombone a little bit, but drums and trumpet was my main influences in music. I played the drums for a while, and then trumpet too, and took the other two instruments along as a general music thing. It worked out pretty good for a while, and then I just went ahead and started catching gigs with different musicians. I played the drums when I could, and did less and less on the trumpet. But I still know the scales on the instrument.

I kind of got into blues by accident. I had started out with the trumpet and drums, and I liked the big band sound, horns and all that stuff. I listened to a lot of records, and the people who I listened to back then were Louis Jordan, T-Bone Walker with the guitar, Wynonie Harris, and then the rest came natural. I kind of gradually got into the blues after I had been spending time in Chicago. I would always rely on learning, getting a great inspiration from the people I would see doing the things I was taught to do.

Like many of the musicians in Chicago, I played on the street. One of the most famous places in Chicago at that time to play was Maxwell Street. Robert Nighthawk, the Howlin' Wolf, Muddy Waters, Little Walter, Robert Lockwood, Jr., Hound Dog Taylor, the whole host of musicians played Maxwell Street. They had matinees on Saturday and Sunday. That was a big thing in the whole area of Chicago because a lot of the musicians that you heard on records, they played on the streets during the daytime to pay their rent and stuff because they made a lot more doing that than when they was playing the clubs.

They would play the clubs at night and some of them, if they had a recording session to do, they would divide it between the clubs, the recording studios, and doing the street scene.

I jumped right into the street scene because it didn't matter what age you was. It was a fight between being a kid going to school during the day and playing in a club like a grown-up at night. But the classroom, and playing on the street, it was a whole different thing. I would play the street when I would be out of my class in the afternoon, and then if I didn't have a heavy assignment or nothing to do, then I would play a club at night. A lot of the students did this, and there was a lot of music played on the school campus. A lot of the guys, that's all they would do. They'd go to school by day and play the clubs at night, and then a lot of them had just certain days when they would go to school. The rest of the time they would have off and do what they wished to do.

That was basically the same as I was, but I really didn't have any real strict assignments that I couldn't get out right away because I had a time of day when I would do certain things. After my classes, if I didn't go right to the street scene, I'd do what studying I had to do. Then I'd go play the streets for maybe a couple or three hours, then go back and do my studying again, then go into a club with a guardian. It wasn't like going to clubs today. Someone in the band would go with me to play, as a guardian to see that nothing happened to me and to vouch for me to get into the clubs.

It wasn't much of a problem to be without good vision in the school. In the music classes, they would play the arrangement for me, and I could do most or maybe all of the stuff from memory. It would look hard, but by me being surrounded by music like I have for the biggest portion of my life, well, it was easy. I was quick to catch on, knowing what the tempos was and the part that I was supposed to play. It really wasn't a big deal. But the biggest problem that I had was playing music with bands that wasn't equally as good as I was, you know what I mean? When they had the sheet music right there in front of them, it looked as if they could just go ahead and jump right into it, because it was right there in front of them to read. But a lot of them would get sidetracked on that. And then a lot of times I would have to catch myself. A lot of them would be wondering how was I doing it, and they'd be concentrating on what I was doing versus what they were supposed to be doing. Saying how could I do this and do it just as good or better than they were doing, and I couldn't see how to read it.

But even nowadays, people look at it like seeing is believing. Well, that's true. But if you depend on your hearing, that's a big, important part also. If you hear an arrangement, you lock that into your mind, then the next few bars of the song or the rest of the song, you have all that locked in, and you don't forget that.

I couldn't have gone on to a musical career if I hadn't attended the American Conservatory of Music. I could have played music, but I couldn't have achieved the career that I have over the years. Piney Woods was at the beginning, and the American Conservatory played a big part in it. It still is one of the most powerful schools for musical knowledge. I was there for four years, but I didn't have any particular instructors that stick out as being that important, because I looked at it like instructors were just being instructors, doing their job.

Of the other students there who had an impact on me, the late Wayne Bennett sticks out. He came from Oklahoma City. He played guitar with Bobby Bland and a lot of other guys, and he did some work with Elmore James. We were close friends. Lou Rawls wasn't a student there, but he was a good friend of mine. Chicago was where he was born and reared. And he was really into gospel. He went out to the West Coast and sang with a group called the Pilgrim Travelers. He would travel back and forth to Chicago from Los Angeles. And there was Sam Cooke, from Clarksdale, Mississippi. At that time, he was singing with a group called the Soul Stirrers. Then they renamed themselves the Chicago Soul Stirrers. He and Lou Rawls were two of my best friends.

In March 1952, I happened to be over at a club called Silvio's when Elmore James dropped in. He had just recorded a Robert Johnson tune that was a big one for him, "Dust My Broom." He was working on some more material, but he couldn't get a drummer to do some gigs with him there in Chicago. A lot of the people who recorded with Elmore had day gigs and recording sessions already booked, so they wouldn't be able to make a tour with him doing the Chittlin' Circuit. So this friend of mine, Odie Payne, he told Elmore, "Now I know a gentleman from Mississippi, he might would take the gig, but you got to treat him right," just like that. Elmore said, "Yeah, man, a guy from Mississippi, you know, naturally I'll look out for him, 'cause that's where I'm from." Odie said, "Well, he could very easily play your stuff. He blows trumpet, too, but you're in search of a drummer." Odie asked me did I want to take a shot at it, and I said, "Well, I'll blast a few with him." So I sat in with him, and that's how I got the gig, playing with Elmore off and on throughout the rest of his whole career.

I did gigs with Elmore for the next four years. We worked around in Chicago and sometimes we went out on the Chittlin' Circuit. Even though I was sixteen or seventeen at this time, I was pretty big for my age, and when me and the band would walk in together, nobody paid me much attention. Sometimes, a club owner might ask about me if he looked and thought I might be a little young. One of the band would vouch for me with a piece of paper saying he was my guardian, and after we paid the union fee, everybody was happy. I never did have to sit out a gig because somebody said I was too young to be in the joint.

As time went by, I guess I was about eighteen or nineteen, I formed my own group called the Windy City Six. I had sat in with different people during a few club dates by then, playing drums and singing. Then I quit playing the drums, and I sang and blew trumpet for a while. We were doing tunes that Louis Jordan and T-Bone Walker did. They were two favorite guys that was in my corner, that stuck in my mind as far as being up into the music world.

We were playing a weekend gig at a club called the White Rose out in Phoenix City, near Chicago, when a well-dressed gentleman walked backstage after we took a break. He booked the clubs and he was also a well-known DJ. His name was Sid McCoy. He came back and said, "Young man, T-Bone Walker was here about six weeks ago. Louis Jordan was here six months ago. Everybody remembers that. You are here tonight and supposedly the whole weekend. Who are you? Oh, I know you are Sam Myers, but musically, who are you?" That put another thorn in my crown, when he asked me that. He said, "Well, I just wanted to give you some food for thought."

I went back and got the guys together in the dressing room. I said, "Now, what we need to do here, y'all play like you been playing all along, we're not really going to be faking nothing. Play the same song, 'Chicken Shack,' and just look to me for the words." I did that and made it into my own song. Another one of them I did, and I very seldom do it now, it's called, "These Young Girls Are About to Drive Me Wild." It was an upbeat thing, swing, and the people went for it. So we did that same show the whole weekend, and on the last night I was coming off stage, getting ready to go back to the dressing room, and Mr. McCoy stopped me in the middle of the floor. He caught my arm and said, "Young man, let's go back to the dressing room, I've got some things I want to pull your coat about." When we got back there, he said, "You did good. What I told you Friday night, it was just something for you to think about. But it seems like you've got everything together. Now, we were talking with your manager and we've got you another booking here starting next week. We've got you three weeks in a row." I said, "Oh, really?" He said, "Yes. What I meant about the music that you were doing, regardless as to what you do by somebody else, it's not yours unless you add your own touch to it. You can't make it your own by doing it the same way somebody else did it. You got to put your own thing to it."

And that stayed with me up until the age that I am now, which is seventy years old. And I've passed that advice along to a lot of musicians: regardless as to what you do by somebody else, or whatever tunes you cover, unless you roll it out in a blanket of your own, you haven't done nothing.

CHAPTER 5

CHICAGO AND JACKSON FAMILIES

Sam's career as an itinerant bluesman didn't lend itself to much of a "normal" family life. But he still found time to fall in love once or twice and even fathered four children. Unfortunately, he has not kept in contact with most for them; he has even lost touch with his son Willie Earl, who lived in Mobile, Alabama, with Sam's father, Ollie, until Ollie had a stroke in 2003. Willie Earl has had some problems with the law, and Sam has lost track of him.

There's a girl who lives in Chicago who I know cared more for me than I really did for her, not that I didn't care for her. Her name is Doris Grisham. We got a little girl together, Sandra Faye, that's our daughter's name. I have four kids all told. I haven't been feeding to the masses a lot, you know; I've planted a few seeds and they came up. That's as close as I ever came to getting married, with Doris. I was too much of a hoofin' horse back then.

I never see my children anymore now. I haven't been in touch with any of my kids in a long time. It's kind of a little hard for me, since I don't deal with e-mails and with writing a lot, and a lot of their telephone numbers I don't even have. That's just the way it goes.

The oldest is Sandra. She should be a little over fifty. She was about the only one who I was really close to. She grew up in Chicago, and later she went to California and Stanford University and became an accountant. The second child was a boy. His name is Willie Earl. His mother was just a chick I was hanging out with. She just got caught up in it and throwed him in my basket, you know. His mama was named Willie Mae Fleming. She's dead now. He's somewhere down in Alabama or Mississippi. I haven't talked to him in a long time. Those two kids are the only ones I was for. The other two, I know them but I don't ever be around them. Their mothers don't blame me and I don't blame them. So I'll just leave it with Sandra and Willie Earl. They are the two who would be present and accounted for just in case that I croak.

My daughter's mother, Doris Grisham, I had a hundred chances to marry her, but I didn't, and right to this day she's not married either. Sandra, the last I heard, she makes her home in California and goes from there back and forth to Chicago. That's where her mom lives. She is the only one of my kids that really seemed like she tried to make something out of herself. I don't know why, but I've just been somewhat like a semi-black sheep to my family. I never was around any of them much, because I was into a whole lot of different stuff than they were. Music is something that has been a very dedicated thing in my life. It's just that I never was around. I went away to school and wasn't around that much. For me, it's been a life like a drifter, so to speak.

Being a musician, I also was a disc jockey, and I met Doris coming out of the radio station one day after she had dropped off some advertising for Spiegel, where she worked. A girl that worked there at the station, they were good friends. This girl was also a DJ. She worked in the office and had a tape commercial for Doris. After I got through doing my show, I came out to the hallway out of the control room, and she introduced me to Doris. I said, "Let me hear that tape commercial you made." She said, "Hmph! He don't seem to be interested in meeting nobody." I said, "No, I just want to hear the commercial. If you have time, I'll talk with you." We just sat and talked for a bit, and we hit it off pretty good. She listened to a lot of music, but I was the first guy that invited her out to where live music was being played. She listened to a lot of records and used to go to a lot of big shows and the opera at the McCormick Convention Center. But to be invited to a jazz club or where they played blues by local people around Chicago, she never did that. I was going to school and working at Chess Records, selling records in their storefront and doing the music scene, too. After about six months we was pretty close to being an item, and she knew nearly every musician that I knew because every time she would come to a club I would introduce her to them. She got to know Willie Dixon pretty good. I wasn't interested in getting married myself, but I asked her one day, "Doris, would you ever get married?" She just told me without even hesitating, "No, and if I don't marry you, I don't guess I'll ever get married. Whatever you do is your business, but I believe that we're going to be together until we decide that we don't get along and don't want one another."

I think a lot about that now.

There was a gal I was seeing besides Doris, and one Sunday we were all getting ready to go to Gary, Indiana. I put my little girl, Sandra, up in the front with Doris, who was driving, and then me and the other woman got in the back seat. I didn't care. We were going along and Doris, I noticed, just kept moving her parasol around, one of them big steel-handled ones. We were coming out of the Dan Ryan Expressway, and in the middle of all the traffic, Doris suddenly pulled over to the side of the road and said, "Get out of the car!" I said, "Oh, why?" She said, "You heard me, get out of the car!" She started crying, and I know there's something wrong whenever you see that woman cry. I was slow about getting out of the car, and she reached back with that durned umbrella and she hit me—whop!—with the steel handle. And even with the way that traffic was moving, the other woman hopped out of the car and just went running. We were going to have a showdown right there, when the woman run off and the little girl hollered, "Run! Run! Run! Run, Miss Mabel, run!" You know how little kids are. Doris said, "Now, get back in the car!" I said, "Well, are we still going on to Gary?" She said, "Yeah, I just wanted to show you that you wasn't as smart as you thought you was." So I got back up in the front seat with her and the little girl, and we went on.

Her mom and I raised Sandra while I was living in Chicago. She was real smart, real good at her books at Austin High School. I don't know to this day how it happened. Austin High was a long ways from the neighborhood where we lived, but she went back and forth to school out there every day. When she was fifteen, she could ride the El and the bus transportation system just like any grown-up could. She was basically a good kid.

The last time I actually saw Sandra was about fifteen years ago. We were playing in Chicago, and she happened to come by the hotel where I was. We couldn't even have dinner or anything together, because I was getting ready to go to the club, and she was getting ready to take a flight back out to California. She was doing good, still single. She said she wasn't interested in getting married right then, no way.

My mother took care of Willie Earl ever since he was six weeks old; he's about forty-five now. Actually, he knows my mother was his grandmother. His mother, Willie Mae, died when he was about ten or eleven. We never were married, but my son always bore my name. We met in Jackson, Mississippi, and that's where Willie Earl was born. I was with Elmore back then, running back and forth to Chicago. We were playing a lot of clubs around Jackson and throughout

Mississippi, and we had our sideline business, the moonshine stuff. Willie Earl was born at the university hospital in Jackson, which is the University Medical Center now. About six weeks after he was born, his mother and I had broke up right before I went out to Texas to do the weekend with a friend of mine, a tenor sax player named Duke Huddleston. I guess he still lives in Dallas; I haven't heard from him in quite a while. I used to come out with him and do gigs. We'd do stuff for the government, a lot of political people. Duke is originally from Jackson, but he's been living out here in Dallas for a long time. He was the first black man to have a TV show in Mississippi. I was working with his group part-time then, too, for a lot of government parties and at the white clubs. That's where the money was really being made by a musician at that time. We played clubs in Jackson like the Wagon Wheel. It was at 104 East Capitol Street, upstairs over a clothing store called R. C. Brown's. We also played at another club on Pearl Street called the Sable Room, not far from the old Jackson Municipal Auditorium.

Because Willie Mae and I had broke up, I was renting from a lady on 127 West Davis Street there in Jackson. While I was in Dallas, I found out Willie Mae was going to give the boy away. Not put him up for adoption, but just give him away. She had had a lot of kids, but she didn't like having any of them around like most people because they cramped her style.

I had called my landlady, Miss Beale, and she said, "You know, if you could get somebody to stand in for you, what you need to do is get home as fast as you can because Willie Mae is fixing to give that boy away." I called my mother and asked her how soon could she get to Jackson. After I told her what was going on, she said, "I could leave Mobile now and be there in about four hours." I said, "If I took a flight out it would take me four hours." Back then they didn't have a jet service going to Jackson. I said, "We going to have to work this out. By the time you get to the house, I'll be there at the same time." So she left Mobile going to Jackson. I told Duke, "I'm going to try to make it back in time for the gig tonight." He said, "Well, you don't have to be there until nine o'clock. But if it's an emergency thing, we could work around you. You'll still get paid."

So I came on home, and when I got there my mama was already there. Willie Mae wanted to know why was I back so early. I told her that I had found out what she was doing. I still had something like a wardrobe trunk there at her place, so I packed the rest of my clothes and stuff and she said, "What you doing?" I said, "I'm moving out of here for good." I put my stuff in that big trunk and left her standing in the doorway crying her eyeballs out. Matter of fact, I took the next evening flight back to Dallas, and I made it to the gig in time. So that was the end of her and me. My mama took Willie Earl back to Mobile with her. So, heck, I didn't care. After I finished my gig with Duke, I came back to Jackson. I already had me another place to live, so that was about it.

Willie Mae was an all right person, but also she was kind of on the rough side. Course, I wasn't no angel then myself, I might say. But it was one of those deals where we really weren't meant to be together. That's what it all boiled down to. Willie Earl would ask me from time to time, "Where's Mother?" I said, "Well, she's not around, son." He wanted to know what she looked like. So one day I finally told him, "We're going to get some pictures together and show you." My mother had some snapshots of Willie Mae and showed them to him, and he told her, "No, that's not my mama, you my mama." So we just left it at that.

I finally told him on his thirtieth birthday that she had got killed in New York around 1970. It didn't bother him much, because he really didn't know her. Another woman had got into it with her, and just beat her doing what she thought she was going to do. Cut her throat,

yeah. Being in a place like New York during that time period, it was
a rough town. She liked to hang around in the saloons and run with
a rough crowd. The only job that she had was working in clubs that
she really liked. She was a good worker, knew a lot of work to do, and
she could always get a job. The nightclub scene, working in bars and
restaurants, that was her type of job. She was a professional shoplifter
as well. I never was in touch with her after we broke up. I happened to
hear about her passing through one of her daughters, Dora Lee. She
told me what had happened and I said, "Well, when you live a fast life,
that's the way it usually comes out." I looked at her like that was not
the kind of life for me, as a man of my ability. But some of the best
clothes I ever wore in my life, she sewed the material and made them
for me. She was a good seamstress. Even with the way that she lived
and stuff, she didn't believe in going hungry and didn't want nobody
around her to be hungry. I think well of her for that.

Naturally I got on with my life, being a musician and all. Just like
I said, it's a way of life. Just one of those things. Years later, after he
became a man, Willie Earl got into trouble, but other than that, things
have been a pretty sweet life for me. I never have been into no real, real
heavy problem things myself, so to speak, so what happened to Willie
Earl really went down into deep stuff.

Willie Earl's been to jail twice. The first time was when he killed
a guy. He had been working with some guys doing some kind of electrical work. Willie Earl and one of the guys didn't get along noway.
They was up at the office, and when the man paid them off, the guy
told Willie Earl that he owed him some money. Willie Earl cashed
his check and gave the guy his money. He had to rush to the house
because he and Mama and Dad were leaving to go up to Mississippi
that weekend. This guy followed him home, and they had some words
about some electrical wire cutters that belonged to my son and this
guy wanted them. He came up in the yard and called him out. When

Willie Earl went out, the guy picked up a shovel, and he broke the handle of it across Willie Earl's head. He was swinging at him again, so Willie Earl took a knife and just plugged him right in the heart.

All of his buddies, they run off and left him. They called the cops, and they put Willie Earl in jail. They had witnesses that saw that this was a self-defense thing, so the cops were just going to hold him for a little while in jail until after the funeral, then turn him out. I was working at the Industries for the Blind there in Jackson, and Mama called me and told me what had happened. I told her, "Whatever you do, don't worry about getting a lawyer." She said, "Well, that's my baby . . . ," you know, this, that, and the other. I said, "Well, I don't care. I've got to tell you this, whatever gonna happen to him gonna happen to him whether you got any money or not. But it don't make no sense for you to spend every dime that you got and when you get broke you find out that he was going to be set free anyway, and the lawyer's done got all your money." So they told her at the jail, "We know this is a self-defense thing, but we're not going to turn him out right now simply because we got to see what his family thinks about it." Come to find out, that boy's family didn't care nothing about him noway. But you know law enforcement works a funny way. Naturally, when they let him out, being in Mobile, Alabama, in the South, once you had a record with the police department, whether it was in a good self-defense or not, you still was a marked person.

A few years later, he had gotten married, and the cops set him up. This woman told him that she was trying to get to her car that had quit on her. He was working at the Oldsmobile dealership there in Mobile, and he had bought him a pickup truck. He was hanging out at this place, and this cop came up, and of all the people that had automobiles there, he was picked to be the fall guy. The cop told him to take her to get her car and see if he could get it fixed for her. He said, "Well, I know a little about mechanics," and he went on around. She dropped a bag of reefer and a bunch of pills on the floorboard of his truck, and when he got out, she had this little scanner, and the other cops pulled up on him and arrested him and took him to jail. He spent two years up north of Mobile at one of those prison farms.

Then Mama really got wired up. She wanted to go and do everything she could to get him out. I said, "Mama, you've got that boy out of practically everything that he got into, but you know lawyers and people like that will drain you for everything you got. He's gotta hit it so he'll know what it is about life. Let this be a learning lesson for him." No, she didn't want to do that. So me and my brothers and sister, we all told her if she messed around and got broke doing what she could for that boy when it didn't make any sense to do it, we would never come again, we'd forget about the family. She started thinking about that, and she didn't do nothing. But she would carry him cigarettes and money and stuff up there on visiting days. But she didn't cut that money loose to try to get him out. He was supposed to do two years, but he got off a year early for good behavior. I said, "Well, that was all the time he was gonna get in the first place. You would have spent every dime that you had, and then when the lawyer find out that you didn't have no more money, he was gonna tell you, 'Well, I did all that I could do.' He can't get but two years, he was gonna do that time anyway." Willie Earl's wife was messin' around. She didn't go to see him any time when he was in jail. First time he ever said anything to me that I thought made sense, he asked me what I would do in a case like that. I said, "Look, you a man, and it's right there in front of you and you don't even see it. I'd forget about her." And so he did, and ever since then, he's been doing all right for himself.

I never did be involved with my other two kids that much because of a whole lot of things that me and their mothers couldn't see eye-to-eye on. So that kind of put a damper on that. I wound up doing a whole lot of different stuff. I just never have been the type person to let things worry me. It just really means a lot to me, to see people doing good. I never liked to hear about anything bad happening to nobody. So, it's just what you go through and deal with in life, I imagine.

I never have been the type of person who wanted to live above my means. I've been a person that's always tried to be a provider for myself. I always wound up trying to deal with getting what I needed to have or the best that I could get, without being wrong about it. It would have to be done in a professional way before it would be right. I was always interested in nothing but what was meant for me. What I mean by being interested in, I don't want anything that doesn't rightfully belong to me. I just wanted to become a good-living person, and over the years, that has been a thing that I eventually wound up achieving.

CHAPTER 6

ELMORE JAMES

Sam's long association with Elmore James was perhaps the most important collaboration of his career. As a youngster of sixteen he met the newly famous Elmore in Chicago a few months after the 1951 release of Elmore's biggest hit, "Dust My Broom." It was recorded at Lillian McMurry's Trumpet Records in Jackson, a studio that in a few years would figure significantly in the life of the young Sam Myers.

Sam was invited to join Elmore's peripatetic group as one of a revolving cast of studio and road drummers on the "Chittlin' Circuit." This was the name given to the loose route that black R&B and blues bands traveled in the 1950s and 1960s, mostly through the Deep South and as far north as Pittsburgh and Detroit. It involved moving from gig to gig in automobiles stuffed with instruments and luggage, and it was a hardscrabble existence for musicians who relied on word of mouth to persuade the next club or theater owner to book them for a night or two. Many owners would even pit one band against another in competitions to see who the crowd wanted to have back again.

Sam appeared on record with Elmore on such songs as "The Sky Is Crying" (Fire Records, 1959), "Stormy Monday" and "Madison Blues" (Chess Records, 1960), "Rollin' and Tumblin'" (Fire, 1960) and a later version of "Dust My Broom" (Enjoy Records, 1963). Their association *lasted until 1963, when Elmore passed away from a heart attack at the age of forty-five.*

Starting off in 1952, Elmore was paying me thirty-five dollars a night, playing drums. During the whole time we worked together, I didn't blow much harp, which is what a lot of people look for me to do now, every time when they see me. I didn't blow harmonica on but two of his recordings. One was a big classic by him, "Look on Yonder Wall." That was on Fire and Fury, Bobby Robinson's label out of New York. We did that one in New Orleans. I played with him from '52 until '63, the time when he died.

"Dust My Broom" was actually a Robert Johnson song, but Elmore had made it into his own by the way he played it, all electrified. It was a big record for him. Big Bill Hill and his brother had a cleaners and a booking agency, Colt's Booking Agency, on Madison Street. Big Bill was a disc jockey and used to do his show from there at the cleaners, through radio station WOPA. A lot of the bluesmen who he booked would have shows on that station. From there he would be playing their records from time to time, being also a booking agent and a promoter and a DJ. They called that "breaking their records," playing their records when they just came out. That's how a lot of them got started.

After a couple more years I had begun to get fed up with Chicago. To me, Chicago was a good opportunity; there was some nice clubs there. But one thing I never did like, whenever you had your own money to spend, you had to hide it away so nobody would know you had any. If you spent any money, they would know you had some, and they would try to get it away from you. It was like there might be somebody watching, and there might not be, but that's the way life had begun to get there. People was always watching you. If you was somewhere by yourself, they'd jackpot you and take everything you had.

That's what the city was known for. It was a harsh life to live. So by 1956 I had got out of Chicago, and I was more or less permanently living in Jackson when I wasn't touring or recording with Elmore.

About 1957, at Vee-Jay Records, Elmore and I did "It Hurts Me Too," "You Know I'm Coming Home," and "The Twelve-Year-Old Boy." The guy that played guitar with Bobby Bland for a long time, the late Wayne Bennett, he was on those sessions. After we went on tour, Big Joe Turner did a couple of songs called "Oke-She-Moke-She-Pop" and "T.V. Mama." It was a Big Joe record for Atlantic Records, but me and Elmore were on the session. In 1959, I was on the session for "The Sky Is Crying," on Fire. Now, there's one thing about Elmore and his recording sessions. He could come out of the studio, and if a guy wanted to record him right across the street or around the corner from where he just came out of the studio, he'd go in and record. A lot of guys would tell him, "Man, you got a big record out there, you're doing good, I'd like to do something with you. But you've already got a contract, you're lined up with this guy." Elmore would say, "When can you get the studio? Do you have a studio already? I can go in whenever you get ready. I just have to get my band together and we can go in and record."

That's the kind of guy he was. What royalties that he did have, it was hard for him to get because he had a lot of records on so many different labels.

After that, he did some more work over at Chess. "Madison Blues," "Can't Hold Out," and "Whose Muddy Shoes." I was on those. There were these guys in California, Joe Bihari and his brother Jules, who had Modern Records out of Los Angeles. Elmore did "Sunnyland" for them. I wasn't on that, but I played it on his shows. What I would do was to listen to the record, and I kept the beat in my head. That's how I would play them on the different shows. A lot of people have asked me, was I on that session? I tell 'em no, but it would have been the same thing if I had said yes, because they were going to say I was there anyway because I was in the band. There was a whole lot of guys in and out of the band with him at the time, but he basically had Johnny Jones on piano, J. T. Brown on tenor sax, and Grady "Fats" Jackson blowing two saxes at the same time. I didn't meet Fats until we did the Big Joe Turner session.

Elmore did a lot of stuff for the Bihari brothers on RPM and a few other labels. What people would do, they would try to capture his music from different gigs, even though he never did do a live album. They would always try to record him on his live shows, but he was against that. On most all of the Bobby Robinson Fire and Fury sessions from 1958 until 1963, I was on a lot of that stuff. We also did sessions in Chicago, New Orleans, and then New York. That was a pretty interesting thing. We recorded "The Sky Is Crying" in Chicago at Chess Studios, but it was on Bobby's Fire and Fury label. A lot of labels did work there, like a lot of stuff they did on Delmark. They figured that by them not having a studio of their own at the time, since they were using Chess Recording Company musicians, why not just go into their studio and do it there? Like Cosimo's in New Orleans, they would lease out to all labels. Johnny Vincent and Ace Records, that's how he did a lot of his stuff out of New Orleans. He would cut it in Jackson at Trumpet and have it pressed down there in New Orleans. He had a lot of Louisiana musicians that he recorded with at Cosimo's. That was the big studio at the time.

Anyway, back to Elmore. He did "The-Twelve-Year-Old Boy," which was a remake. I was in the studio at the time, but I wasn't playing drums on that one. But the first one, with Wayne Bennett, I was on that. That's kind of a strange song. The story behind that, there was a kid who used to hang around Elmore's house. The woman, she just liked youngsters, like most women of today. But twelve years old, that's mighty small at that time period. He mentioned that the young boy used to hang around his house until late hours of the night, and he wouldn't have thought with a kid that young that she would have in mind to treat him right. In the song he says, "If a young boy hangs around, you should do what I should have did, send him over to your neighbor's, and hope your neighbor likes kids." That was just a wild thing. Elmore should have been doing his homework, yeah. He just wasn't thinking. He was probably looking for a place to make some whiskey, or was heading out the door to a gig.

We had some good times together, in and out of the studio. Elmore recorded "Dust My Broom" over a dozen times with different labels. He really had an identifying thing with his slide guitar, though. A lot of guys played slide, but the minute that he put that slide on his finger and ran it across those strings, you would know it was him doing it. We used to play a lot out at one of Percy Simpson's clubs in Jackson, Mr. P's. It wasn't a really big club, but it was nice-sized. They had gambling facilities in the back, and guys would come there just to gamble. While they would gamble, their lady friends would stay up front and listen to the music. Boy, there was a lot of gamblers who lost their women up in there! Lost their money and their women. But it was a real nice place to play. That club was the highlight of Jackson for a long time until they went out of business. They moved it and changed it to Club 77. If you knew we were going to be playing there on the weekend at ten o'clock, you had to get there about seven to get a good seat. They kept a thriving business, so we would play there on Wednesday, Friday, Saturday, and Sunday night whenever we was in town. It was just a home-based gig for us.

Being as Elmore was originally from Mississippi, we would always come back to Jackson when we wasn't on the road. He'd get some bookings from his recording company, but back then they didn't have too many agents that would go to bat for him. That's where we would remain, in Jackson, until we hit the road again. Sometimes Elmore would do recordings with the same people he traveled with, and sometimes he would record with a lot of different people. But he would always try to record with the same people he traveled with.

Elmore was a nice guy to be around. He wasn't a flashy guy; he didn't have a lot of ego. People who'd be talking to him that did have ego, the first thing he'd say to them was, "It's good that the world is not full of people like you. There's enough room out here for everybody." Those would be his words. "Don't think you're so great that you can't respect your fellow man." He was the kind of person, if he had anything that you needed, he'd let you have it. What was so strange about him, if he was broke, he wouldn't take nothing from you. I never could understand that about him.

He always would tell me, "Man, you know what, you should never worry. If somebody who owes you is in business, you always got a shot at 'em. But the person who you should worry about is the son of a gun who owes you and won't pay you and he's going out of business. That's the one that's really getting over on you, you know." And that's true.

Elmore and I ran a little sideline together back in Mississippi. We had us a still on the banks of the Pearl River in Jackson, right across from the Stillwell Reservoir, where the floodgates were in that north corner. What was good about that spot was that you had swift running water, and anywhere you had a fast stream of clear running water, that's where you made your best whiskey. We were right at the spillway, leading from the river into the reservoir. Right there at that spot, there was a guy that was working for the company that was building it. He was a good friend with us, and he gave us the layout with the map and everything that they were going to do. So we never did get caught while we had our still, but a lot of people around us did. There was a revenue man named Sam Newman. He said if anybody was making whiskey anywhere in the state of Mississippi, he would catch 'em. But he never did catch us.

We went in it, not blindfolded, and we got out of it at the right time. What would happen, when we were off the road, we'd be in there making whiskey. The way we would do it, we had a lady that would help us. We called her "Big Mama." She took our orders, plus she sold the whiskey for us. Then we had a couple of guys in the police department to keep stuff down, to let us know what was happening. We had our airtight thing, you know? My deal was, before we would go to the still, I'd make it my business to go down to the corner of Monument and Farish Street there in Jackson to see what I could hear. There was this black guy, Jake, that ran with the revenue guy, Sam Newman. Jake would be down there on the corner talking about the stills they hit. "Every one of you guys, you have it good, I didn't get in until about four o'clock this morning. We was off in Rankin County . . . ," and all that sort of stuff.

We had a smart thing going on while we was in the whiskey-making business. There was a guy on the police force who was really sick. I had always told him that I'd like to have his radio. He went into the hospital, and he never did come out. That radio was one of the things among his personal things that didn't nobody get, because I stole it. We could get a frequency on the highway patrol, the sheriff of Hinds County, and even the city cops. And I had to be careful about carrying it to a radio shop. I had some work I needed to have done on the durn thing, but I knew a guy who had his own business on Mill Street. He knew the kind of radio it was, but he fixed it for me. And I used to just turn the thing on and listen to police calls, the wrecks on the highway, and the stuff that the deputy sheriffs was doing even long after that. When you had tubes that would be gone bad, you had to be careful about that. You had to really be on the watch as to what you were doing. But the way I had that thing fixed up after I got it, there would've been no way, unless they were special looking for it, for them to have been able to find out what it was. I even had it painted a different color, and where the name of the radio was, I had taped over it. If anybody saw it and if I didn't have it on, they'd just think it was a ham radio. I kept that radio a long while.

One time, they almost caught us. I don't know if someone tipped them off to where the still was or if they were just wandering blind. This guy Newman had all different kinds of ways to catch people selling whiskey. Now where we was, there wasn't no cattle over there. But he put a cowbell around his neck and he'd be walkin' along. If anybody heard it, they'd think it'd be a cow, and before they'd know anything, he'd be up on 'em. So we had our setup going, everything cooking and slowin' and goin' in a hidden deal by some brushwood. A person could walk by it all day long, and if they didn't see nobody out there, if it wasn't operating they wouldn't even know it was there. So, in the middle of a conversation Elmore and me was having, I heard something. We both had a rifle apiece; I had a .30-30 Winchester and I was as good a shot as anybody else. What a lot of people don't know right today that knows how to use weapons, what would make it more accurate for you to hit your target, you got to be able to hear as well as to see.

I said, "Man, somebody's cow must've got out over here." He said, "There ain't no cows within miles of this place." And there wasn't, because from where we was, far from any settlement where people lived, they had nothing but a big steel mill. So Elmore said, "Man, you hearing things, there must be something back in Chicago on your mind." I said, "No, hell, it ain't either, my mind's right here in these woods. Did you see that light flash?" He said, "You gotta be crazy now, 'cause there's not even lightning." I said, "That wasn't what it looked like. It looked like it was some kind of a flashlight." He looked and he saw it and he said, "Damn, I must be going crazy, too, 'cause I saw it then. I hear a bell, it went ding-ding-ding-ding." I said, "Yeah, do you want to know something about it?" He said, "What's that?" I said, "Did you know a cowbell don't ring up high? It ring down low." He said,

"That do sound strange." I said, "Yeah." He said, "Hot dog, I heard it again." I said, "Well, I heard it too. It's either we gettin' wild amongst one another in these woods or somebody's coming up on us." He said, "No, hell, you right, I see the light now." And he was about as far from us as about a hundred feet. Elmore said, "Man, put out the fire and let's get up this shit and get out of here!" I said, "Well, before we do that, that's Sam Newman, I know it is. We could kill that SOB and won't nobody know that we did it." I reversed the rifle, and just then Elmore said, "Hey, man, put out the goddam fire, put out the fire!" I put the fire out and I said, "You see the light now, don't you?" He said, "Yeah. They right here on us!" I said, "Well, I'm going to pick him off!" He said, "Man, put that rifle down and let's go!" And so I put it back in position and we took off running. And they got about as close from me as ten feet but they couldn't see us. We could see him 'cause he was running blind in the dark, too. They had those flashlights, but that brushwood kept 'em from seeing who we was, and we run until we got up on the highway. I said, "Yes sir, here that son of a gun's truck is, parked right behind us."

Where he messed up at, he did not do like a lot of people did back then; he didn't fix our truck to where we couldn't leave. They probably was waitin' for us to run for it, they thought they were going to catch us right at the deal. And we had fake tags, too. Back during that time they had license plates where you could switch license plates and have another state's tag under your own. It could be the same truck. When you're doing stuff illegal, you gotta do every illegal aspect that you can. We threw our stuff in the back, put our rifles up in the rack over our heads and jumped in. The truck just went, "Ummmmmmm!" Now, that durn truck had been cranking ever since before then. I said, "Oh, hell, man, we better hurry up and do something because they coming up in the highway." And just at the time when Newman's foot hit the pavement, that durn motor turned over—rhoom!—so we took off. And they shot at us, they might have killed us, but they had pistols. If they had rifles like we had, they could have shot us up. But I wanted to shoot that man, though. I really did.

The next morning I went down on the corner to select information. Newman's guy Jake said, "Man, you know what, last night we was over on the Fannin Road in Rankin County. I don't know who it was but we almost caught 'em." I said, "Yeah? What happened?" He said, "Well, we parked behind 'em, it was a blue Ford. I think I know whose it was, but I'm not saying." I said, "Well, there's a lot of blue Fords around here." He said, "Yeah, but there is only one particular truck that's like it." Then he didn't want to talk about it any more. I said to myself, yeah, you black son of a bitch, you almost got killed and didn't even know it. So that's the closest we ever come to being caught. We used to go back and forth to the still in that durn truck.

We gave a guy six hundred dollars for it. He said, "Well, I need some money, that's the reason why I'm lettin' y'all have it. But I used this truck to run whiskey." I said, "Woodrow, you a friend of mine, and I don't want you to say nothing about this, but what the hell do you think we want the truck for?" He said, "That's what I figured you want it for. But if there's anything ever happen, I want that truck back." I said, "Twelve hundred bucks and you can get it back whenever we go out of business."

There was this one guy who we got our copper coil pipes from at the Jackson Iron & Metal Company on Rankin Street, in south Jackson. We used to make whiskey for him because he let us have that pipe for free, more or less. When we decided that we were getting out of the whiskey business, he gave us a thousand dollars for the copper. That was good money back then. And we had about two hundred-something gallons of liquor that was left over. He said, "I'll give you fifteen dollars for every gallon you got." We said, "Do you want us to cut that copper up?" He said, "No, don't cut it up." Normally you'd think if you were working at an iron and metal company like him, he would cut it up himself. He sent some men over, and the only thing they cut was the pipes from them tanks so they could get it onto their truck. And when they brought that durn truck in on the day that he paid us off, I noticed he didn't park the truck in the line on the crushing side where they have the welding torches and the cutters. He had it parked over on the other side of the yard.

After he paid us for the still, he gave us the fifteen dollars for every gallon of the leftover whiskey that we had. He wanted to know, did we want that in separate checks? We said, "You just add it up and just make us one check." He said, "Well, I'll just go ahead and pay you cash money for this," and so he did. We asked him, "Hey, man, we've got a flaming cutting torch, we could cut the thing up for you." No, he didn't want to cut it up. We pointed the copper out to him where it was. Course, he had been there and saw our operation so many times, he was the one who gave us the copper coil pipe and the stuff to join 'em off to get the still going. He used one of the company trucks to pick the copper up. He had a truck that was big enough; he could just load the whole thing on it without even cutting it up.

I happened to be thinking about it one night after it was over with. We were rooming with a guy named Johnny Temple. We were sitting watching TV, getting ready to go to work out at Percy Simpson's place. I said, "Elmore, don't you think it would be strange for a person, if they was in the iron business and was going to buy some iron, why they wouldn't just crush it with all the rest of the iron?" He said, "Well, that might have been his personal thing." I said, "Yeah, it was. I bet you that guy might go into a business of his own." He said, "Well, no doubt he would. Hell, he paid for it, so what can you say?" So after Elmore had passed, I found out that the guy had retired from the Jackson Iron & Metal Company. Years later I saw him in Lynchburg, Tennessee. He had gotten government approval to make whiskey for the Tennessee distilleries, to make Jack Daniel's. I had thought it was kind of strange that he didn't put the pipe from that still over with the rest of the iron. He just piled that truck over by itself, away from that area. And so that's the way it went.

With Elmore, we toured and played on what they called the Chittlin' Circuit through the South. We went to Camden, Texas, a couple of times. We never did go to Austin or Dallas, but we would always go to Houston. That would be the main city that we would play, and then we would go up into southwest Louisiana and come back. There was the Satellite Club and the Golden Key Ballroom in Houston. All those are gone now, all those clubs up and down the Fifth Ward in Houston. I used to hang out at a lot of them. Don Robey was a big wheel back then; he had the Duke Recording Company. Duke, Sure Shot, Peacock, and Back Beat, those were his labels. We'd play at a lot of his clubs there, in and around Houston.

Back when I was playing drums with Elmore, I never did loan my drums to anybody. But if we were working on a gig or a session, if a guy didn't want to set his drums up and mine was set up and he wanted to play them, he was welcome to do so. I've always been funny about that. If I were there to lend a helping hand to any musician, I would do that. I once had a set of Rogers Black Pearls. I was working with Elmore, and Odie Payne used to tell me all the time, "Man, you know you've got about the sharpest set around." I had all these different strobe lights and stuff on them and when I hit the stage, I'd just flip a switch. I could switch them to a stroll, or if I wanted the lights to be moving with the tempo of the music that was playing, I could do that, too. A lot of guys thought it was a cool thing, and they respected me. They wouldn't play my drums like they was driving a nail through a board with the sticks. And they sounded good, playing.

Odie said, "One day, I'm going to own them drums." I said, "Well, according to whoever's going to be the longest liver." Just like that, just joking with him. But I got into some trouble, I fell down and needed a hand out and took 'em to a pawnshop. That set of drums had cost me fifteen hundred dollars. Odie took it upon himself to find out where my drums went. He found out where I pawned the drums, and he went down there and switched the durn pawn ticket and got 'em out before the date I was supposed to get 'em out. I had told the guy I'd come back and get 'em. I had pawned 'em for a thousand. But Odie went and paid the guy like sixteen hundred. You know how a pawnbroker can do stuff. But I messed around and didn't pursue it after he got the drums. He said, "You can play 'em anytime." I said, "Okay," but I wasn't thinking right and I went and tore the durn pawn ticket up. What I should've done is went before a lawyer and sued the durn pawnshop. The ticket was all I needed. But that's how a lot of those guys, especially around Chicago, stayed in business. Odie's daughter has still got that same set of drums now. We stayed good friends; I didn't think nothing of it. In this day and time, what a person would do, they probably would really go over the edge. But we never stopped speaking with one another or nothing like that.

We were getting ready to go overseas in 1963 when Elmore passed. We had been touring all down through Mississippi, and then he went back to Chicago to get the overseas tour ready. I got my passport and stuff what I would need to go, and I was supposed to join him in Chicago that Monday. He was rehearsing with some more musicians in Chicago that was going on the tour with us, but I was going to be the one to play drums. This made me think he kind of knew he wouldn't be living long, because before he left, he said something to the club owner where we played in Jackson, Mississippi. It was a place called the S&S, owned by Percy Simpson, out on Moonbeam Street. Elmore told him, "Look, we're going to see about getting this tour together, but if things happen, if anything happens to me and you're still in business, I want Sam to have a job. Would you make me that promise?" So after he passed, as long as Percy was in business, I played at his club. You know, a weekend gig. But I had the option of doing my own thing, just so I let him know ahead of time, but I always had a gig whenever I came back to Jackson. I left and went overseas, this was in '64, and when I came back, he was out of business. His nephew John Simpson said, "We still got the club. Do you want to work?" I said, "Well, I'm working out alone." He said, "Sure, I understand what you mean, but you got the gig if you want it." Percy Simpson had died and John had taken over the club, but it still held on, and I played around. I'd run to Atlanta, maybe to Florida, but whenever I came back I still had a gig at the club.

CHAPTER 7

JACKSON, MISSISSIPPI

Jackson, Mississippi, was originally a trading post on the west bank of the Pearl River in a spot known as LeFleur's Bluff. Named for President Andrew Jackson, the little town was designated as the state capital in 1821 due to its abundant timber, attractive countryside, and proximity to navigable waters. In 1839, the first law in the United States granting property rights to married women was passed there. Burned three times during the Civil War, Jackson had a population of only eight thousand at the turn of the century. The advent of the modern railroads after World War I fueled the rapid growth in the timber industry in that part of the state, and the opening of a large (for the region) airport propelled Jackson towards the modern age.

I was living permanently in Jackson by 1956, rooming with a friend of mine, Johnny Temple. Johnny had lived in Chicago for about twenty-three years, where he was a big figure in the music field as a guitar player. He did a couple of recordings called "Big Boat Whistle" and "New Vicksburg Blues" for the Decca record people. His career extended on blues, and he played a lot of orchestration-type stuff, the big band arrangements. He'd strum chords with that, but he actually played a lot of lead guitar with his blues. He wasn't a big influence on me; I just loved working with him, and I liked the sound of his voice when he'd be singing. I never did any recordings with him, but I did do some gigs with him while he and I were with King Mose and the Royal Rockers.

When Johnny's mother passed in 1952, he moved back to Jackson from Chicago to take care of her house. When I was with King Mose there in Jackson, I started rooming at Johnny's house with my lady friend. I never will forget the house where he lived because the address was 905 Anne Banks Street, right off of Whitfield Mills Road. That's what it was known as then. I lived with him from 1957 until about 1960. It was a real nice, big house and he had a garden in the back that he worked every day. He did his own cooking, and he was a master of the kitchen. We would have lots of fun during the day. When I wasn't on the road traveling with King Mose, one thing I used to enjoy was making ice cream. Johnny had an old ice cream maker, one of those with a handle you would turn, and we made a lot of ice cream.

Elmore James had gotten out of the hospital in Chicago in 1957, and he came down to live with Johnny. We were just like one big family. Elmore used to fix gumbo and eggnog. It was a great time we all spent together. Johnny Temple, we all called him Temple, he would be getting those royalty checks from the Decca record people and a lot of other people who he had recorded material with, so he had enough money to get by on pretty well, with the three of us also living there. It was just a joyous time.

Temple was a real nice man, and he would do what he could to help someone. It was in 1958 when my son was born. Once he got sick with diarrhea when I was out on the road. My son's mother didn't have any transportation, and it was late at night. I think that the fee to be admitted to the emergency room then was five dollars. Temple got his car and took my son's mother and him to the hospital. When I got home, I went to pay him his money back. He said, "Oh, man, you don't owe me nothin'. That's the way life is. You may be able to do something for me, one day." Just like that. I still insisted on paying him. By him taking the boy to the hospital and what he had spent, I took it to be a life saver for him.

Another time, I forget what year it was, but it was in the summer. Elmore came in and he made a big pot of gumbo. After he got the gumbo cooking and going on, he told Temple, "Now, don't let it cook too long, because it will get mushy." Elmore went on out hunting; he loved to hunt and fish. Temple got himself a big bowl of gumbo, and then he fed the rest of it to his neighbors. They all thought he was the one who had fixed it. A while later, Elmore came back, and I looked for him to be really pissed off about it, but he didn't say anything, and neither did Johnny. It was just one of those things. After Temple passed in 1968, somehow they tore the house down. Every time when I would go back to Jackson, I would look for that particular house, knowing it's not there.

Not long after I got back to Jackson, when I wasn't playing a gig with Elmore, I started running the road, doing my own thing with my own band that I put together. It was called the Shades of Rhythm, with Jimmie King on vocals, Freddie Waite on drums, and Leon Dixon, Willie Dixon's nephew, on bass. We also had Jesse James Russell; we called him "Lightnin'." He was on guitar, and Walter Berry was on piano. I was singing and blowing harmonica. We was together from 1956 to about 1958. Then I went to do a recording thing with Bobby Robinson, since Elmore had vouched for me to record something of my own with Bobby. On a couple of the sessions Elmore played guitar on some of it, so I began to make a name from that. I was interviewed by a lot of magazines and began to get it together then. In 1959 and 1960, when we did the records with Bobby Robinson, there was "Sad, Sad Lonesome Day," "You Don't Have to Go," "Poor Little Angel Child," "Little Girl," and I did one called "Sad and Lonesome." "You

Don't Have to Go" and "Sad, Sad Lonesome Day" had the late Dave Campbell from Jackson on piano and "King Mose" Taylor on drums. Matter of fact, it was Mose's band who were the session guys. "Poor Little Angel Child" and "Little Girl" was recorded with Elmore's group, but King Mose was playing drums on that. "Big Moose" Walker was on piano, Sammy Lee Bulley was on bass and I was on vocal. It was two different outfits there. And then after that, I've just drifted from recording company to recording company.

King Mose died of leukemia a week after Elmore passed, around the first of June 1963, and he was buried on the fourth. I stayed on with Johnny for a while longer, and then I moved out to what is called west Jackson. For the next three years or so, I traveled all over, coming back to play in Jackson whenever I could. If I wanted to be there for a weekend, I had a club where I could go over and play, and I also did hotel gigs. I would always pick up a little session work and I worked pretty steady, even with things being like they were. When I had a hotel gig, I was working six nights a week. In 1965 I went overseas with a blues tour run by a lady out of Chicago named Sylvia Embry. I was out of the country for about eighteen months. The band was made up of different guys from different groups, sort of an all-star deal. She was married then to John Embry, a guitar player on that tour. We went a whole lot of places, kind of like an international world tour. When I came back, I started back playing around Jackson again with a few different groups and on my own, doing my weekend deals. I'd run up to Chicago, do a lot of different stuff. But a lot of the clubs closed, and some of them moved out to the North Side.

The blues was going into a stage like a depression, and I was looking for job security, so I wound up getting this job at the Industries for the Blind in Jackson. If it worked out that I lived long enough to retire, I would have worked under the Social Security law and got my pension built up. So with that happening, it wound up being a pretty

good little thing there. I worked five days, sometimes seven days on
my job at the Industries for the Blind. But I was still doing music at
the same time, and that's why I always say that music has played a big
part in my life.

I worked all over that place, since I had better vision then. I
worked in the shipping department and the mop department. It was a
manufacturing factory deal. They made brooms, mops, gun belts for
the military, barracks bags, inner springs, box springs, a whole lot of
different stuff. This plant was connected with the National Industries
for the Blind in New York. There were twenty-seven of those plants,
and the wage and pay scale and benefits at the plant in Jackson was
number one over all of them. But there was a few supervisors working
there that I didn't see eye-to-eye with. It wasn't that they didn't have
the work to be done. It was just that there were people there that I
couldn't get along with.

I worked there at the Industries for the Blind for fifteen and a
half of the thirty years in all that I lived in Jackson. But I would still
do a lot of weekends at different places. I would get a leave of absence
from my day job and I would go and do my engagements. By 1970 I
had been working about four years at the Industries for the Blind. I
was playing a lot at the Sunset Inn, on the same street where Percy
Simpson's place was. I did some gigs there with one of my groups, the
Downbeats. We had a guy in it named Robert Miller. I left and told
him to take the band over. I left for a little bit, and then came back
and just let him handle the management of it because I had got fed up
with that stuff. That's when I was working with him over at Foster's
Nightclub. That was on Blair Street, right around the corner where I
lived at the time, on Monument.

I had another group called the Blue Light Blues Band, from about
1968 to about 1972. We played a lot at a club there in Jackson called
the Lamar. It was a theater that they had converted into a club. In that

band with me was James Russell, the same guy that played guitar with me on a lot of that Fire and Fury stuff that I recorded under my name. We had Walter Berry on piano and Leon Dixon on guitar and on bass. I had Sherman Norwood on drums, and I was singing. We played frat parties throughout the south, up at Ole Miss (the University of Mississippi), Mississippi State, at the Holiday Inn in Columbus, then down at Mississippi Southern in Hattiesburg, and just all around. Mel Brown took a break from Bobby Bland, and he worked with me for a while. That was the only band that I had under my management.

In about 1972 I started working with the Sound Corporation. That was Willie Silars, he was the drummer, and Pete Garland on piano. Jesse Robinson was on guitar. Charles Fairlee would come up from Moss Point, near the Pascagoula area. He would come up and do a lot of weekend stuff with us. He was on tenor sax. We did the Elks Club, the Palm Garden, clubs like that in Jackson that was happening at that time. There was another club I played at over in Lula, Mississippi, called the Push N' Pull Club. That was with a bunch of different guys out of Greenville, places like that. The bass player was George Allen. He was the studio bass player at Malaco for a long time. He would do sessions with Johnny Barranco and all of them over at Malaco. They was really kickin' in high cotton back then. I never did nothing for them, recording-wise. We'd play in other places like Talullah, Louisiana, doing pickup gigs around the Delta area.

In 1979 I went back overseas with the Mississippi Delta Blues Band. It was different guys, most of them were from California; I was the only guy from Mississippi. Bob Deance, guitar; Richard Milton, drums; Gary Asazawa, he was on rhythm guitar. Norman Hill was another bass player. The second time around was Bob Deance, Richard Milton, and Craig Horton also on guitar. Craig was a really good guitarist and songwriter, but the rest of the band wasn't about nothing. We had another guy, his name was Haskell Sadler, out of

Oakland. We all called him "Cool Papa." He was a durned good guitar player, too. He died here recently; he was a good man. That brings it up to about 1982, when I did the World's Fair with Robert Lockwood, Jr., in Knoxville, Tennessee, in summer of 1982. It was about that time I met Anson when he was playing over at the George Street Grocery in Jackson.

Overall, the Industries for the Blind was a decent place to work. But you had a lot of people, just like the NAACP, they had a lot of blacks really wanting to get positions and stuff. On jobs like that, they usually call those people "cheese-eaters." They were always going to the man in the office, telling him about what one person wasn't doing. They had a meeting once and I mentioned that, and they all got messed off with me. One of the guys just got highly pissed about my ideas about things. Right about then I happened to be in New Orleans in 1984 during the World's Fair, doing some work for the state of Mississippi as one of the representatives of the entertainment department. Since I had to get a leave of absence from my job to go do these gigs, I'd have someone from the head office to contact the people at the plant and give me a letter of recommendation to go do these things, and everything would work out fine. Whenever I got ready to leave, I always was able to just go into what I wanted to do. The manager told me, "You can just go when you want to," but I told him it's always best to get permission before you do anything.

The last time I was there at the factory, I was making nine hundred dollars a week from the World's Fair, cash money, and I wasn't working as long or as hard. When I came back to work, there was a big write-up in the paper about me with a picture of the work that I did at the World's Fair. Then I made a commercial on TV about the Mississippi travel ticket, as to when you go to the World's Fair you should always travel through Mississippi. From the way it was set up, regardless to where you were coming from, going to New Orleans from the east, you would have to come through Mississippi. After I made that TV thing, people got to seeing it. The little kids on the street, I'd be walking, and they'd say, "Oh, we saw you on TV!" I'd say, "Oh, really?" and they'd say, "Yeah, 'It's a Treat to Even Sleep in the Mississippi Sun,' ha ha ha!" and they'd be laughing like I did on the commercial. And I'd say, "Oh, yeah!" That made me feel good, that people who didn't even know me would always come up doing that. I had felt like I had done something for somebody.

During the World's Fair, I had a week's break and flew out to Dallas to do a recording session with Anson Funderburgh. That album, *My Love Is Here to Stay*, on the Black Top record label, was my first one with Anson. So after I did that, I went back to New Orleans and worked some more for the Mississippi Expo at the World's Fair. I got to thinking, since I had finished up that Sunday and it had been a while since I rode a train, I took the train back home to Jackson and went to work that Monday morning. People were looking at all this stuff in the paper about me. And you know how people will be talking on the job, "Well, this guy is traveling more than the people that work in the offices here, he's doing this, he's doing that, he's doing better than the rest of us." And they got to talking that around the area where I worked at. I didn't want to hear stuff like that, so what I did, and it was the wrong thing to do, but I did it anyway. I quit. I didn't even let the people in the office know I was leaving.

I caught the Greyhound bus that night and went back to New Orleans and then worked the whole season of the World's Fair out down there. My supervisor at that time said, "Man, if you're gonna leave, you should tell somebody something." I said, "I'm not letting anybody know a damn thing," just like that. Course, I was making more money doing what I was doing at the World's Fair, but when that ran out, that wasn't what I was thinking about. The idea was just making that money. So I got paid for this recording session with

Anson, and then I came back to Jackson and started doing some of the same stuff I usually did around there, playing in different clubs and doing more stuff musically.

Anson had heard of my work from a long time back, in 1982. They were playing a club in Jackson called the George Street Grocery. It was a grocery store at one time, and then it was converted into a club. The upstairs part used to be a warehouse for the store. They built a restaurant and bar downstairs and just a bar upstairs. That's where the music would be. When Anson and the boys came through to play, I happened to be in town, and I went out and sat in with them, and we hit it off from that. He asked me about joining the group in April 1986, and that's where I've been since.

I didn't look for it to last as long as it has. But I look at it like, hey, you know, at age seventy, if a man don't know what he wants to do in this time, there's no need of him being here. I'd like for my opinion or my ideas to be heard whether there's anything did about them or not. I always believe in doing things that makes me happy. My motto that I live by, if you don't do the things that makes you happy, you're not doing a thing except making yourself miserable and the people around you miserable. That's a sad gathering there, I think.

CHAPTER 8

JACKSON RADIO AND RECORDING

In the mid-1950s the music scene in Jackson, Mississippi, was thriving. Black culture was centered on what is now known as the Farish Street Historical District. It took its name from a former slave, Walter Farish, who had settled at the corner of what became Farish and Davis streets. Blues music had long been an important part of Jackson's history, beginning with furniture store owner H. C. Speir, who moved his business onto Farish Street in 1925. Speir was interested in music and scouted for local talent. In those days, furniture stores sold record players, and their owners sometimes promoted local artists as an inducement for people to buy the record players. Speir ran a sideline business making test recordings; he made several of some now famous blues artists such as Ishmon Bracey, Tommy Johnson, Charley Patton, and Skip James. He provided the means and connections to have their songs recorded by Victor and Paramount after they auditioned for him in his furniture store. He similarly assisted with the early careers of Willie Brown, Son House, and Robert Johnson by recommending them to labels like Vocalion. Speir closed down his music business in 1944 during the musician union's strike against the major record companies.

Speir was soon followed by Willard and Lillian McMurry. The young
couple started the Trumpet record label in 1949, recording mostly gospel
music until Sonny Boy Williamson II (Rice Miller) joined the label. His
great popularity paved the way for other blues artists of the day to record
at Trumpet. Also on the label was Elmore James, who later would some-
times be backed by a young drummer named Sammy Myers (Sam did
not play on any of James's Trumpet sides).

Another person of stature in the Jackson music world was Johnny
Vincent. He would also influence Sam's career, though not in the way
that Sam would have preferred. Vincent did engineering work for
Trumpet and started his own label, Ace Records, in 1955. He leased
masters of recordings by Elmore James and Sonny Boy Williamson II
from Trumpet and rereleased them on the Ace label. Vincent went on to
discover and record a number of other popular blues, R&B, and coun-
try and western artists of the era. Sam recorded his most famous single,
"Sleeping in the Ground," for Ace in December 1956.

Jackson also boasted the oldest black radio station in the state,
WOKJ. Sam resumed his radio career there in 1956.

In Jackson, Mississippi, I was a disc jockey at WOKJ radio. We would
play from record players, and a guy would set up a mic so you would
have a speaker that you could hear as you went along. That's why it
was so easy for me to be as active as I was in radio. I never did do any
news or stuff like that; that was the hardest part, back during that
time, to read the news. There were a whole lot of guys who were top
disc jockeys that didn't do the news. They always had somebody else
to do it, on the hour or five minutes before the hour. Nine times out
of ten, the person who did the news would be the person whose next
show was coming up, unless the next person's show lasted past the
hour. Course, they could have a person from the newsroom to do it,
and sometimes the engineerman would do it. Most of the radio back

then was just like working on a job where you did your work manually. You were your own engineerman, you'd spin your records, and you operated everything yourself. Now, the commercials that I did, a lot of them were in Braille. I did most of my reading from Braille, but I still had the same time period to do certain things like anybody else would, like stopping to make an announcement between songs.

The guy that owned the station where I worked at, John McLendon, he had about four radio stations. The one I worked at was WOKJ in Jackson, Mississippi, the first black radio station in the state. It started off in 1947 with five thousand watts of power, and then it went to fifty thousand. It was on the dial at 1590 when they started, then in 1965 it moved to 1550 when they went to fifty thousand watts. Amongst the DJs that they had at that time that I worked real close with was a gentleman from Vicksburg, Mississippi, named Bruce Payne. He had been working in Birmingham, Alabama, at one of their sister stations, the main one, WENN. It's called "WIN Radio." All these stations were connected with what was called the "Ebony Network." They also had KOKY in Little Rock, Arkansas, and KOKA in Shreveport, Louisiana. Later on, they opened a station in Tampa, Florida, WYOU.

That all happened from 1954 to 1955, along back during the time when I was still in Chicago. I came to work there at WOKJ in April '56, after I moved back to Jackson. I was hired on as a DJ, but by me being a musician, they knew that I would have gigs that I'd be doing on the Chittlin' Circuit. So they gave me a time slot for my show where on the weekends, if I wanted to be off, I could be off. My regular thing was from Monday through Friday if I was in town. If they had a special event going on, like if it was football season, they'd have someone to do my show for me up until game time if I was away.

At this time, I was working with King Mose and the Royal Rockers. I would come down to the station, and the guys would already be there. I played some songs with them on the air and did the announcing for the band like when and where we would be performing. We didn't have a sponsor at first. Then the show got so good that a supermarket sponsored us. It came to be a chain, but at first it was just one grocery store called the New Deal Supermarket. It was on the corner of Church and Farish streets in Jackson. They moved from that store years later into a bigger one. Down south of Jackson at Crystal Springs, on the way to New Orleans, they opened a new store. They built it from the ground up, a great big one. They were our sponsors for a long time.

On Saturdays, the department of parks and recreation would put on a show from noon to about five in the evening. The whole Jackson scene of musicians, if they wanted to play on the radio, they came out to the College Park Auditorium. It was located in College Park off of Lynch Street, about three or four blocks west of Jackson State University. They would follow my portion of the show, which was on from nine-thirty until noon. They had another disc jockey, Jody Martin, who was called "the Tall Man." He would be at the auditorium getting ready to bring on the show from there. King Mose and the Royal Rockers didn't come on until whenever I got there from the station, which was right down the street. When I'd sign off my show at twelve o'clock on Saturdays I would say, "Now through the remote facilities of WOKJ, we take you to the College Park Auditorium, where your announcer for the extravaganza for the next three hours will be your host, Jody Martin." Then I'd switch the remote on, and he'd cut in and start talking and then bring up the first band.

It was a great thing, being in radio. I enjoyed it just as much as I did playing music, simply because I learned one thing: as far as working equipment, you could be the greatest person out there to do that. You could tear down a transmitter and you could put it back together. You could be that good, but until you learned one thing that has to do with common courtesy and common knowledge, until you learn to talk to who you're performing to, radio or musically, you haven't done nothing. Music can be played from now on, but if you're the host at any function, a DJ or whatever, you haven't done nothing until you've learned how to talk to your fellow man. That rode with me in a lot of ways. Even right today, when I'm on a stage with my band or with anybody else's band that I'm working with, I feel that it's important to involve whoever your audience is into what you're doing. It makes them feel better, which a lot of musicians today you don't find doing that.

I did the DJ thing for about four or five years. About thirty-five or maybe forty years later, when I went back to Jackson after being with Anson for a long stretch, they gave me an honorary stone celebration thing. It's a stone plaque with my likeness on it that they're going to put in what's called the "Walk of Fame" on Farish Street in Jackson. I was overwhelmed; it really made me feel good about having that happen. I was proud to see a couple of people that had gone into retirement, but they came out just for that day. These were people that I hardly even said anything to when I was in radio. You know, you do your show, "Hey, man, I'm outta here!" "All right, how ya doin', we'll see you around some, uh-huh." People who you never just sat with and had a really long conversation. A lot of these people said even though they were all full-time professional DJs, they learned a lot from Sam Myers. It really made me feel good to know that. I don't think they've put the plaque in the street yet, but that is a project that's in the making. They even gave me a small copy of the plaque to hang on my wall.

One guy who was honored that day is not alive. His name was Rice Miller, who a lot of people call Sonny Boy Williamson II. It was almost like they reopened the doors of the Trumpet record company, Miss Lillian McMurry's company, where Sonny Boy had recorded a lot. They honored him on that day and then Dorothy Moore and myself. Miss Lillian's daughter accepted the award for Sonny Boy. It really surprised me. She is a young woman now and probably has a family of her own. After the awards ceremony, I walked her out in front of the theater and they were all taking pictures. She said, "You know, it seems like a dream, but I remember you." I said, "It don't seem that it was that long ago, I remember when you was a little girl, being up to the studio with your mother." She said she could kind of remember that. I said, "I understand how over the years, things can stay with you."

It wasn't all that unusual for a white woman to be running a studio recording black musicians in Mississippi. There were a lot of guys that had studios and they had women working for them, but she had her own company and studio. Miss Lillian really did something for the music in Mississippi during that time. Even though she was the head person there, she had blacks and whites working for her. The late Johnny Vincent was one of her engineermen. He had his own record store called Johnny's Records. Even after he got his own label, Ace Records, he used to record a lot of his artists there at her studio. Musicians like Willie Love, Sonny Boy Williamson II, and a group called the Seven Sons, which was a gospel group, and a guy from over in Meridian, Sherman "Blues" Johnson. Most everybody in Mississippi recorded there. Little Milton didn't record under his name there, but he was on a lot of the recording sessions that she did.

In December of 1956, at 309 North Farish Street at the Trumpet recording company studio in Jackson, Mississippi, I did "Sleeping in the Ground" and "My Love Is Here to Stay." Johnny Vincent was the engineerman of that session, and it went on his label, Ace Records. The number of that particular song was 536. I recorded it, and he paid me and the rest of the band twenty-five dollars apiece. That was the only money I ever got out of that song. No royalties, just the session fee. This is how the song went:

I would rather see you
Sleeping in the ground,
I would rather see you

Sleeping in the ground
Than to stay around here
If you're gonna put me down.

Well, I give you all my money,
Everything I own.
Well, I give you all my money,
Everything I own.
Well, some day I'm gonna get lucky,
And down the road you know I'm goin'.

Well, I would rather see you
Sleeping in the ground,
Well, I would rather see you
Sleeping in the ground
Than to stay around here
If you're gonna put me down.

You know I give you all my money,
Yeah little girl, everything I own.
Well, I give you all my money,
Everything I own.
Well, today I'm gonna get lucky,
And down the road you know I'm goin'.

[1956, words and music by Sam Myers]

The people who played on it was King Mose Taylor on drums, Walter Berry was on piano. He later became a doctor and retired from the University Medical Center in Jackson. Walter Crowley, a brick mason, he was on bass. The guitar player, who is no longer with us, was Tommy Lee Thompson. All he did was music. And myself on vocals and harmonica, that was the group. It was a big record because like most records back then, it was released quickly and radio stations were playing it by the month of February 1957. We had gone over to the studio on a Sunday night, but we didn't get a chance to record anything, because he had several other musicians there who had been recording for him long before I was. On Wednesday, we recorded it. I never did receive any royalties, not even from Johnny Vincent. He'd say, "Hey, man, you got a pretty big record out there. I'm proud of my label for doing it. Do you need anything?" And he would give me five, maybe ten bucks. I wouldn't consider that as being royalties because he never gave me a statement. He was like a lot of people in the recording industry that had artists back then. It was like it was just this little bitty record, and he never thought about it until he saw you. Instead of sitting down like a gentleman and making a royalty statement and a check special to me, he just said, "Here, put this cash in your pocket." He had told me the royalty was going to be 2 percent of the record sales. But the twenty-five-dollar session fee and some pocket change now and then was all he ever paid me. He just never did anything with the royalties. Dave Campbell was a classical and jazz piano player who used to direct Miss McMurry's music department on her label. Dave took the song and wrote it out into sheet music for the session. But what he did, unbeknownst to me, was to put the song in as being published by him. In later years, he sold it to some guy in England. He didn't put anybody else's name on it, he just said he owned it, and that was good enough as far as anybody else was concerned.

I wish a lot of Texas guys could have got a chance to really get into the real thing, the way they played the blues back in Chicago during that time. They probably wouldn't be so hung up on what they think they know now. But music has changed a whole lot since then, a whole lot. I was talking with Mel Brown when I was up in Canada recording my CD, remembering back when Miss Lillian McMurry was recording in her studio at Trumpet Records. They wasn't paying the guys much money, but the more songs you had, the more that she would pay you. But she tried to cut you low on that, too. She'd get a stool and be sitting with a short dress pulled up. When come time to pay the guys for the session, it wasn't but ten dollars. She would do that stuff just to keep from paying the guy, distracting him that way. She was a good-looking young woman then, in her thirties, maybe close to forty. But overall, something good came out of it.

Trumpet was *the* recording company back during those days. She did gospel, did a whole lot of stuff. B.B. used to record there, but he didn't do no stuff under his name. If he was going to be playing a gig in Jackson, he'd come down to the studios and lay down a few tracks. He knew most of the guys, and he would take his guitar and strum through some stuff with them. Rice Miller, he was in some of those sessions. He did a song called "From the Bottom." He and B.B. were big buddies, and B.B. played guitar on that. You'd be surprised at a lot of those guys, how they survived a lot of that stuff and who are still around. But the majority of them are gone.

It was a very interesting thing, and I would play a lot of their music on my radio show. I had a thing that I was gonna do on one of my shows, and we was just about to get it hooked up, but then I just up and left the station. They didn't fire me; I just up and left. But I came up with a good excuse, which they bought, and it was good for me. What it was, I decided that I'd like to hit the road again and do nothing but music. That's the way I left it. But there were a lot of guys in and out of that station, WOKJ, when I was there. It was the only station in Jackson that played a lot of R&B and gospel. I had a whole lot of friends that worked there. They would ship a lot of the DJs around to different places, but they never really got around to doing me that way because I had quit. I just decided it was time for me to do something different.

CHAPTER 9

THE BLUES

What is the meaning of the blues? How does it feel to have the blues?
What's it like to listen to the blues? There are as many answers to ques-
tions like these as there are blues fans, scholars, and musicians. Everyone
hears and understands the blues in a different way. A student of the blues
could spend the rest of his or her life reading, researching, writing, and
talking about the blues and barely scratch the surface of this deep subject.
So, what does one do to try to gain an understanding of the blues? There
is really no firm answer, except for what one finds within one's own soul
that resonates to the blues. Or, one can seek out a blues artist, a longtime
practitioner of the art and member of a dwindling generation that will
all too soon be lost to history as age and time finally take their toll. Here,
Sam expresses his feelings on what the blues means to him, discusses
some notable blues musicians and blues styles, and describes his unique
song-writing process.

Now I'll talk about the blues and what the blues means to me. I looked
at the blues for a long time before even studying its contents. To me,
people often look at blues as being depressing and about hardships.
Well, that's true. But there are three known directions blues can go
in. One, there are some happy blues, and then there are blues where

you have problems, to where you can't see your economic situation. And then it can be just a story sung musically about the facts of life. It don't always have to be about a woman. It could be something that happened to you, or it could be something that you've seen happen to someone else. I've heard it said, and I go along with it, that it takes a worried man to sing a worried song, but that's not always the blues. It's the way you feel about it, the way you express it.

The blues is really expressing in a musical story form the way you feel about something. And in order for it to go over big for you, you have to have a feeling for what you're doing. That's what it really means to me. And it's not all of the time that the words of a song should rhyme. It would be better if it did rhyme, but it's just like telling a story. It's a very simple thing, but people look at it as being hard. But it really is a simple thing, that's why you have a lot of music that is being played right today that got its start from the blues. And it's just telling a true story about the facts of life, the hardships. Or maybe in some ways, it's a story about that you are happy. Usually, a blues song is about a woman. If it's a blues song, in order to make it a happy blues song, it's in the way that you do your phrasing: "Yes, this chick is coming back, I'm a happy man, I feel like a millionaire even if I don't have a dime." By the same token, you might feel good, but even millionaires have the blues. Where their blues starts, people might say, "Look at that guy standing over there by that Lexus." "Who you mean, the guy by the Chevrolet pickup?" "No, the one that's right next to the Mercedes-Benz. That guy's got plenty money." So many ways he's got money, but he also got blues. Where his blues begins versus a person that don't have money, his blues begins when he had to get lawyers that he pays a lot of money for him to keep what he's got. Where, vice versa, a person that don't have much, he might be having to scuffle up what he needs to eat or where he needs to live. That's where would I say even rich people have the blues, because they try to scheme and connive to keep what they have. You've never heard of a person that was being sued unless there was a lot of money involved. That's where your blues starts. Basically, it's when you don't have something you need, or it's something that could be handled in a way that you could still have it and still be blue.

I hear people look at Monday like it's supposed to be a blue day, "Blue Monday." Well, you're not always supposed to look at Monday as being a hangover from Sunday night's party. You could be blue in a lot of ways come Monday. Maybe you're not able to work things out on Monday that you need to work out. Well, you see, you're blue about it. And that same thing could not only be on Monday, it could be Tuesday, Wednesday, Thursday, Friday, or Saturday. So that's my pronunciation of the blues and what it's all about.

A really great blues song has certain things about it. Not only could it be something that happened to you, it could be something that you see happening in everyday life. It could be the problems of a neighbor, or somebody who you see who had something happen to them in the streets. It could revolve with people all around you. Whether it's a sad blues or if it just rambles on slow, it could still be a good feeling. It's not always something bad that you see happen, or something that has happened to you, like a relationship with a lady. Anything can turn to blues. It just goes with the flow of the facts of life.

Fast and happy songs, like in swing and jump blues, also fit into the blues world. You could be doing some swing blues: "For you my love, I'll do most anything." You know, you're happy and you feel free in doing this. Or you have had hardships for a number of days, weeks, months, or maybe a year, and all of a sudden you're happy because you got a telephone call or maybe a letter that the one that you dearly love is coming home. So, it is in a blues perspective, but you are happy about it.

A good example of a great blues musician who could bring out that kind of emotion would be one of the world's greatest as he is known today. He's a guitarist and he's recognized. The person that I'm speaking about is known to be one of the world's greatest at this sort of thing. That would be B.B. King, because to my knowledge he can do all styles of blues. The next person who also can do that is Bobby Bland. You've got what is called hard-core blues. It can go from that to blues tradition. The way it is today, both of those guys are the greatest to me as being vocalists, even though B.B. plays his instrument. They can take today's music to any level. I would say that those two would be the ones who are alive today, who really have been able to polish that off.

You see, years ago, people looked at blues as being about hard times when it's really not that way. Blues can come to you in different forms, like when most women sing about the losing of their old man and men speak about the loss of their lady. But that's just one way of the blues. It's a simple thing; you can be happy and have the blues. A lot of people don't believe that. But basically, what the blues can really turn you into a hard-boiled case is, when you broke, you have got nothing but blues. When you're broke, you're down and out, you can't see nowhere can you get ahead, well, you're blue. I wish people would stop saying the blues is a good man gone bad. It's not that, it's more like a good man feeling bad. Naturally, it's part of it when you're broke and can see no way out. Naturally you feel bad about it; you got blues. But there's a blues of happiness as well. Also, people have gotten to where they've run out of old standard names of music. You even got stuff now, like rap, it has began to catch on real good. For just throwing something together, I would say it's doing pretty good. Now they've got a new thing called hip-hop, and no one can explain to me what is meant by that, "hip-hop." What're you doing, you just hipping and hopping?

But the old standards are blues, gospel, and jazz. And now, they have even turned gospel music around so it is called contemporary gospel. There is a Top 40 thing in gospel like there is in the Top 40 charts in *Billboard* magazine. You've even got Christian rock and Christian blues. That's where you run out of names. Christian is Christian and blues is blues. It's more related to gospel than to anything else because you're singing about Christianity. I know a lot of the quartets have big orchestras backing them up doing gospel, but it sounds like they're doing a disco song. The only way you can really understand what's happening is when they sing, "Oh, Lord!" or "My Savior!" or something like that. But otherwise, you wouldn't know it from anything else.

I believe there is such a thing as Mississippi Delta blues, because it bends back towards slavery more than anything else. But whether it's Texas blues or Chicago blues, they're just names that people are throwing out there. Maybe that's just a way to identify the musicians who are from that area. If they are playing Texas blues, they're maybe a Texas person. But, what do you think about a man playing "Scratch My Back"? That was a tune that was written by Slim Harpo. Would you call that Texas blues? I don't think you'd even have to hear it to answer that. Because you would know that Slim Harpo was the first one that did it, and he was originally from Louisiana.

From the beginning, you've got people who are copying stuff that T-Bone Walker and B.B. King did. Now here's what happened to that: all the bluesmen, even B.B., was somewhat influenced by T-Bone. That's what people start out working on, influences, but it don't have to be just that type of blues that they are playing, like Texas blues. Just because a person is from Texas, that don't mean that he plays Texas blues. If Freddie King was still alive and playing, no doubt if his style didn't change he would be playing Mississippi Delta blues. But he was originally a guy from Texas. So the question still remains unanswered to me.

A lot of people hear a song and they say, "Oh, that's Texas blues." What is Texas blues? The only definement that I could find of Texas blues is just Texas blues musicians playing blues, captivating it as being their own. The people who originally did the song that they are covering are miles away from here. Some of them have never even played in Texas. T-Bone, when he went to California to play in Les Hite's band, he definitely didn't play Texas blues into that. But when he started doing his own thing, a lot of people called him Texas blues because they knew he was from Texas. What it was, T-Bone played a whole lot of different stuff as well as his own and he was, I would consider being, a blues musician from Texas. But he definitely wasn't Texas blues like Mance Lipscomb and Lightnin' Hopkins. Lightnin' was from Texas, but he wrote a lot of songs for Delta blues musicians like Muddy Waters and all those cats. Lightnin' wasn't what you'd consider Texas blues either. It's way over my head what Texas blues really is. I think a lot of musicians say, "It's just a name." I go along with what a lot of what people say, but when it comes to having a theory, I have my own beliefs and doubts about it. There are a lot of people who play blues and have gotten away with it over the years, playing the blues and they don't even really know what it is. They don't even know the meaning of it when it's right there in front of them.

You hear a lot of people talk about "West Coast blues," but you never hear anybody say "East Coast blues." You have Piedmont blues, which is close to the East Coast, but the Piedmont style of playing blues is acoustic. One of the greatest things from that area, there are more people playing blues on the East Coast than on the West Coast, like in Boston but not so much of it around New York. Guys do a lot of old blues standards, mostly Piedmont style. As a matter of fact, they do more blues in that part of the country than they do in the whole state of California, but yet you got "West Coast blues." But if it's acoustic, somehow it all comes under the heading of Piedmont. If that's the case, there was Big Bill Broonzy, a gentleman from Arkansas who lived in Chicago for a number of years. That's where he died. He played a lot of acoustic stuff that they called country blues. So why haven't you ever heard of a large quantity of musicians that came from the part of the country that Big Bill Broonzy came from? He was from Arkansas, and as many blues musicians as you have in Arkansas, you never hear about them being from there, 'lessen they get on with a big major label somewhere else.

Like this guy, Michael Burks, who signed with Alligator, he's from Fayetteville, Arkansas. He has a whole lot of guys mixed up in his strings on guitar. Part of it is B.B., and then Albert King. He has established himself real well, but the reason why a lot of people don't recognize him as a heavy-duty bluesman is because of these different styles he's got mixed into one. I don't know how they do it, but a lot of people are being paraded for what name they have and not by what they can do. Elvis Presley was like that, everybody looked at him like he was the king. But what they failed to realize at that time, even though he was a showman in the stuff that he liked to do, it was a black man, Arthur "Big Boy" Crudup, who inspired Elvis how to play guitar. Elvis even recorded several of Arthur's tunes. But the gentleman who was playing the guitar on all that solo work, that fancy fingerpicking stuff, it wasn't Elvis doing that. That was a guy out of Memphis, Scotty Moore. Scotty didn't get a lot of the credit that was due him because people kept hollering, "Elvis is the king! That guy could sure play that guitar!"

John Hammond, Jr., has acclaimed a lot of stuff, and he's good with it. He can do acoustic, and then a band can come onstage and he could play with them. A lot of guys who play acoustic cannot work with a band, because they're used to being solo. That goes with the feeling of what they know to do. Robert Lockwood, Jr., can go both ways. He can do more with a twelve-string guitar than a lot of guys

can with six, 'cause he carries his rhythm, his chords, and his lead
notes all the same. He could take his guitar and do whatever he wants.
A lot of guys play guitar and got big names, but they can only do so
much. I feel like if a man presents himself as a guitar player, he should
be able to do more than just one thing. He's gotta have enough weight
about himself. If he knows his instrument, he should be able to get out
there, and if something goes wrong with the band, he can do something to keep them afloat. If a guy takes his guitar and can't play with
nobody but just the band, he's just somebody living off a pole that
somebody else has notched.

Chords are a very important thing in music with any instrument
that you play, unless it's a saxophone. A saxophone goes to harmony,
but you can balance a chord out by a group of horns playing harmony.
Not the same note, that would be what is called "in unison." But to
harmonize, you pick a part that will blend in with a guy that's playing
the lead. If you could strum up some harmony at the same time when
the guitarist is playing chords, it really helps it out a whole lot.

B.B. knows a lot of chords, but he'll tell you himself, he can't
play and strum chords all at the same time. A lot of times when
B.B. is playing, he may have the guitar on the intro, the solo, and on
the going out. In between, just playing regular chords, he don't do
it. He usually stands there and sings and claps. But that's the way his
style is rounded. He can play one of the best arrangements of "Going
Home" on a guitar that I've ever heard. One night, he walked into Don
Robey's studio there in Houston. They happened to be playing there
that night, just a bunch of musicians getting together and jamming.
Not like the amateur jams you see in Dallas, these were professional
guys going to the test. A guy picks a tune and the band goes off and
plays, and each guy takes a solo to the fullest of what he knows. So
B.B. walks in, sits down, and listens a minute. Then he reaches over
and grabs a guitar, and everybody looks at him, because he's supposed

to know what he's doing. But he decided he would give them a little more something to worry about. The horns were doing their part, then he went off to do his solo, and he did about two things in one. When he got ready to modulate to the song he was gonna do, he just did a lot of stuff like fast notes and running chords. He even did "Tiger Rag." Everybody said, "Now this cat is playing this stuff like he'd been doing it all his life." But that wasn't the point. What he knows, and the way his style was, he had to study that. He had studied music in that form. That's why it was so easy for him to do it.

Count Basie was the first guy to acclaim B.B. as the world's greatest. B.B. made some appearances with Count Basie for a while. People would look at him like, "That's just a guy on stage playing jazz." Now B.B. could play jazz as well as he could the blues. He might be on stage just like one of the guys in the band, with a uniform on. Then when he came out again he'd be dressed different and be like wildfire, which is great. I could understand what he was reaching. If an idea comes to you, you should just go ahead and do it right then, because if you mess around, you'll forget it. Just do it while it's there in front of you. That's why B.B. does what he does so well. Freddie King was a good Texas guitar player, but like I always have said, to hear some good B.B. King music played, I like to hear him do it.

The late Little Milton used to be the same way. For years, before he found out that he could have a thriving style of his own, everything that he played was just like what B.B. King did. Until he found out he could be Little Milton, that's the only way he did it. But just like a lot of guys tell you, "Yeah, man, I gotta start somewhere." But, hell, you don't have to keep that up the rest of your life!

Not only Milton, there were a lot of guys who played guitar and were some pretty decent singers. B.B. was kind of a milestone for a lot of them for a long time, including Buddy Guy. I thought it was a great thing when Milton decided to do his own styling thing. Since he did that, he wound up getting more work, and his popularity began to grow strong; there are just a lot of good things to be said about that. I've known both guys for quite a while and I thought it was a great thing that Milton went on to achieve his own style of performing. It really helped him a lot.

Ever since day one, there have been a lot of people, even if they have a style directly of their own, they usually had a tendency to copy off the other person before they went into their own thing. But a lot of them who started out that way never changed. They grew to be old men and their styles stayed the same. There's a gentleman called "Guitar Gable." There's so many people who sounded like him, until you never knew who was who, because they not only sounded like him, they used the same name. I know of about three or four Guitar Gables. The original was a blues guitarist who also played a lot of other stuff. But there were so many people playing the type of material that he played, until you didn't know one from the other. Like "Guitar Junior" that played with Muddy Waters for a long time, that was his key signature. His real name was Luther Johnson. There were a lot of guys who called themselves Guitar Junior. Clarence Garlow was sometimes called Guitar Junior. He was out of Louisiana. Lonnie Brooks was from Louisiana, too. He was Guitar Junior at one time when he was a young man. But he wound up saying, "Hey, this not going to work." He came out, left the name Guitar Junior alone and went into who he really is, Lonnie Brooks.

So you had a lot of guys who would take the same name. They were copying one another and then they would use that name and would say, "You've heard this guy. Now I'm going to show you where I can do better." Kind of step the style up, while still wearing the name. It's just one of those things. Something else that was interesting about that, there was a harmonica player named Sonny Boy Williamson. The original Sonny Boy was John Lee Williamson. He got killed in Chicago in a knife stabbing. Sonny Boy Number Two, as they would call him, his name was Rice Miller. He hung around mostly the Mississippi Delta, then over at Helena, Arkansas. And even though as flat and as country as he would talk at times, he wrote some good songs. He was a DJ and he just traveled around. How he got to be worldwidely known, he would always travel from town to town, state to state, anywhere, just him and his harmonica. Plus he did a lot of recordings, did a lot of stuff on radio. He was successful at that because the real Sonny Boy, John Lee Williamson, was dead; he had done all his recording back in the forties. Rice Miller had taken the name "Sonny Boy Williamson" even before the original Sonny Boy had died. But after John Lee died, it was wide open for Rice Miller to start calling himself "the original Sonny Boy Williamson."

Rice Miller would come to Chicago to record. He would use the same musicians that Little Walter used. But he didn't stay nowhere long. He didn't care for Chicago, and he had a lot of enemies there. A lot of people didn't like the idea of him taking the name Sonny Boy, when it was originally John Lee Williamson. How he did it, he got his ID and everything to read Sonny Boy Williamson. People who knew him said, "Man, you are not the original Sonny Boy." He'd pull them aside and tell them, "Don't say nothing. I've got a gig to play, then I'm on to the next town." A lot of people around Chicago didn't like that and didn't care for him being around, although he blowed a harp like a demon. He could just pick up and start blowing any style. He never did use much amplified stuff, mostly studio mics. People were pissed off at him, but nobody wanted to hurt him because he blowed stuff that John Lee Williamson didn't blow. Not only did he take the name, he took the music and did something more with it.

He didn't stay long in Chicago, not because he was afraid of anybody, but so he could keep his reputation. Elmore James, Robert Junior, they liked Sonny Boy real good because if he ever got into a contest, he could protect himself with what he know as a musician. Whenever Sonny Boy went to Chicago where the musicians were, that son of a gun, if he walked into a club and if there was any harmonica players there, they just sat back in a corner and watched. And a lot of people don't know that James Cotton used to stay with Sonny Boy when they was in Helena. From a little boy on, Sonny Boy taught James how to blow harmonica. That's why James is as good as he is, right today. I met Rice Miller a few times, had a few laughs with him, but I never did play with him. During that time, I wasn't really all the way interested in harp myself; I was still carrying the trumpet as my main instrument.

Rice Miller also recorded in Jackson, Mississippi, on the Trumpet Records label for Miss Lillian McMurry, in the same studio where I first recorded "My Love Is Here to Stay" and "Sleeping in the Ground." But he was there before I was. The first record that he did on Trumpet in about 1951 was "Eyesight to the Blind," just him, a drummer, and a piano player. From that he did "West Memphis Blues" and "Cool, Cool Blues." He had a piano player, Willie Love, with him at that time that played on his records. He had a group called Willie Love and the Three Aces. Not the Aces out of Chicago, but the Three Aces. Sonny Boy was a part of that, plus he played a lot with the King Biscuit Boys. They consisted of Dudlow Taylor, James Curtis, Robert Lockwood, Jr., and himself. What they would do, they had a broadcast out of Helena, Arkansas, on KFFA, which today they honor every year. The King Biscuit Flour Company has a festival called the King Biscuit Blues Festival in honor of Sonny Boy Williamson because he spent a lot of time in Helena being broadcast on KFFA. Sonny Payne, we all called him "Sunshine" Sonny Payne, he still does that show every day from twelve o'clock until twelve-fifteen. It was back in the forties when he started that, about 1941 or so. The King Biscuit Flour Company started making this meal called Sonny Boy Meal. It was a sack of cornmeal with a picture of him on the bag, which I thought was an honorary thing. And every year since the King Biscuit Blues Festival started, they always bring back Robert Lockwood, Jr., and honor him because he was a member of that band. Then they got a Sonny Boy Blues Museum in Helena and a Sonny Boy Blues Society. I have a plaque that shows where I'm an honorary member, and I really appreciated that. This year, 2005, will be the twentieth year they have been doing it, and me and Anson have done all of them since they started.

I'll tell you what made me be a proud turkey. Out of all the musicians that were there at King Biscuit, anybody that was there at the last one saw that Robert Lockwood, Jr.'s band was uniformed to dress. It's a proud thing for me to say. I wasn't dressed like his musicians, but I was the only one in my band that had a suit on. That made me feel really good. I said, "Hey, this is the blues!" Regardless as to how you were dressed when you got there, if you're going to perform before your audience, you should look presentable. It don't have to be a uniform, but when you have a suit on and you're onstage, you've got that professional look. You're in your working clothes then. When I walk through a crowd, it makes me feel good to have them say, "Hey, man, you sure look nice." Then I know I have truly laid a mark for myself.

After Robert Lockwood, Jr., left Helena, he moved up to St. Louis and then went on to Chicago. Then Joe Willie Wilkins came in, and he and Sonny Boy kept the group going. Then Joe Willie moved from Helena over to Memphis, and he played around there, still using that name, the King Biscuit Boys. He was a real good guitarist, and he also worked with Willie Love. They did a lot of sessions at Miss McMurry's Trumpet studio there in Jackson. A lot of Sonny Boy's records, Willie Love was on them, then he had some sessions that he did on his own. Stuff like "Little Car Blues," "Shout Brother Shout," "Nelson Street Blues" and "74 Blues." A lot of people listening at that song couldn't understand what was "74." Was it just a number? But "74" was the number of a freight train. He mentioned, "74 rolls right by my baby's door / I'm going to hobo my way to Chicago / And I won't be coming back no more." I had a lot of those records. He died at the VA hospital, Willie Love did, in Jackson, Mississippi, in 1953. He had a cousin, Clayton Love, who worked with Ike Turner out of Clarksdale. I never got a chance to meet Willie Love personally, but I really have enjoyed his music because he used the right musicians to make his stuff work for him. A lot of musicians today just get a lot of guys and throw something together, just because it seems it might work. A lot of music from the early days is being covered by up-and-coming people. But if you ever knew the song, it would be a hard thing to recognize it when somebody else plays it, versus going back and listening to the original.

Getting back to Little Milton for a minute, a lot of those sessions he did, he was with Willie Love before he went over to Sun Records out of Memphis. That was his claim to fame, and he was in the business for about fifty years. I think he really made a big mark for himself. To me, he was a good musician, a good guitar player, he was smooth, and he was a hellacious singer. He could sing any kind of music that was around. I never heard him do gospel, though. I'm pretty sure he could have if he had chosen to.

The late Willie Dixon, who's originally from Vicksburg, Mississippi, his regular gig after he disbanded the Big Three Trio was working with Peter Chatman, who the world knows as Memphis Slim. He and Willie used to work together a lot at the 708 Club, the Trianon Ballroom, the Zanzibar, some of the same clubs that Muddy Waters used to work. That was Willie's regular gig when he wasn't doing his own thing, and he was always in the studio doing sessions. A lot of people like Chester Burnett as the Howlin' Wolf and Muddy Waters, all those guys over there at Chess, when they came in, a lot of them wanted to record but didn't have any material. Willie would tell them, "If you want to record, be at the studio at such-and-such a time and such-and-such a date." They'd say, "Man, I wouldn't know what the hell to record, I don't have any material." He'd say, "You just be there, you don't even have to bring your guitar, whichever instrument you play, you don't even have to bring it, unless you feel comfortable in playing it." Willie had a lot of songs and even supplied a lot of the musicians with instruments to do their sessions over at Chess. That's how they all made it.

There were a lot of blues musicians, if they were around today, you would be proud of them. Around the Memphis area, they still don't get a lot of what was due them. Guys like Joe Hill Louis. He used to have a radio show that came on WDIA there in Memphis. It was called "Wheelin' on Beale" and it was done by a man named Ford Nelson. He played the piano there, and he's still part-time at WDIA, doing a lot of gospel stuff on Sundays. He's retired, but he's sort of like Rufus Thomas was. Rufus would do this gospel show in the mornings from around six o'clock 'til around ten, when they started broadcasting their remotes from the different church services. Joe Hill Louis had the name "The One-Man Band," because he had a drum he would play, a bass drum, and he played guitar and a harmonica. He would sing, and he had a rack that went around his neck for his harp. And he would do that, like Jimmy Reed used to do on some of his shows, just sit down and play his guitar. That's when blues was the big thing. Then along came B.B., and after that, a lot of guys just took the blues and swung it with a big band sound. That is called pioneering stuff.

I've been asked a lot of times how do I compare today's music with the early days. It would be hard to really give a close-in opinion, because everybody's trying to sound like the next person. Like people would say, you could be doing your own thing but they like to sort of characterize you with somebody else: "Well, that might be yours, but you sound like Bobby Bland or Wynonie Harris or T-Bone Walker."

They are always there to characterize you instead of to say, "Hey, man, do it the way you feel it." It's always good to think somebody'll hold out a hand or you admire this person's way of doing things, whether there was a style development or not. All that's good, but you can overdo things sometimes. Like a lot of today's music, for instance, it can be overproduced. People like to have onstage what they use in the studio to record with. It's a real simple thing, like when you pass a note or a diagram or a sheet to a sound person to what to use. You could cut that stuff raw and for all the added sounds and stuff, just pass it to the engineer. That's when he goes to work. From the way it's all recorded now, all an engineerman has to do is just switch the machine on, if he got the levels and everything set. You could just record it raw and later on add on all this other stuff. Pretty soon it's the engineerman who's making your record. He can make it or break it. It's almost like it's the record companies that're making the records, not the musicians.

I never thought much of a person who can see you onstage and watch how you are operating your instrument, and after you get through playing the instrument, then you gotta stand around and talk about it with him all night. I've never been that way. But it works for some, and for some, it don't. Some people can do it forever. I don't see no reason why they should, but that's the way they do it. They want to see what kind of amplifier you're playing through, see what kind of guitar you have. You find that amongst guitarists more than you do any other instrument. Saxophone players, wind instruments, they do their thing, then they all may go talk about some arrangement, but they don't go, "Man, why do your horn sound different from mine?" You never have that said, simply because you're a different person even though you're playing the same instrument. There's gotta be something different, even if it's nothing but the tone. But if it blends in together, and it works with what's going on, hey, you did a milestone.

A lot of times people will ask me, why do I cover this song or that song, instead of doing something original. Covering songs is something I never did like to do, but if I happened to cover something that somebody else did, I always liked to put some emphasis on it to make it my own. But after that, I might want to do a song of my own making. The way I would go about writing a song, it don't have to be, but it could be, about something you see happen to a woman and a man. Or you could be down on your luck. Or it could be about a little funny thing that you see happen to somebody else. To keep from forgetting it, I would jot it down in my mind. If I see something else that strikes my attention, I get it written down by somebody right away, and I keep on working on it until I get to what I think is the perfect song.

I was able to use either a typewriter or a Braille writer to write down my songs. I had learned to type on both when I was at Piney Woods. Then I would get somebody to help me. I would read out loud what I wrote down in Braille, and they would copy it down by hand or with a typewriter. But lately I haven't felt up to writing it down myself, so I would get someone to copy it down for me. I would just tell them the song lyrics, and they'd write it down. How I'd remember a song, I'd sing it to myself so many times until I got it locked in, that this is what I'm going to remember. I did all of it from memory.

The main thing is, whatever you do, use your strongest effort to try to make it better. I may go through ten or twenty pages to write one song, but that's what it boils down to. A lot of musicians will use a piano or a guitar or some kind of instrument to help them work up a song. But I do it different. I don't even use a harp. I just mostly would hum the melody to myself and work up the instrumentation later on with who I'm going to get to do it with me.

One of the writers for *Southwest Blues* magazine here in Dallas, Miss Joanna Iz, helped me to prepare all seven original songs I did on my new CD. It's called *Coming from the Old School*. When I went into the studio at Electro-Fi Records up in Canada to record the CD, I would hum the music line to the band and just sing the words. I already had the melody in my head, and they would pick it up. We would work up the arrangements from there. It took us only three days to record that CD.

It was a lot different when I recorded some albums for TJ Records. That was Tom Boyd's label, back more than twenty years ago. On the first one, it was just me and a friend of mine, Tommy Lee Thompson. I played harp and sang, and he played the guitar. It was called *Down Home in Mississippi*. The engineerman had one of those portable studio things, and we went over to Tommy Lee Thompson's house and recorded these songs out in his garage. "Bad Acting Woman" was one of them, and then I did a couple of instrumental things on the chromatic. Later on Tom took it back to California where he was living to mix it and put it on a record. It did about as well as it could, with just the two of us. I did about three or four more with his company. Now, he's not even in the business anymore. The last I heard, he was a computer programmer out in Palo Alto, California.

CHAPTER 10

THE HARMONICA

Even though Sam started out playing the trumpet and the drums, he is now far better known as one of the blues world's premier harmonica players. He received the W. C. Handy award in 1988 for Blues Instrumentalist of the Year—Other (Harmonica). The harmonica, or harp as it is more commonly known in the blues, is a deceptively simple instrument. Because of its small size and the way it is played, the observer often cannot really discern just how a harp player is applying a given technique. The observer can only rely on his or her ears to tell if what the harp player is doing is to the listener's taste. This chapter delves into some of the intricacies of Sam's harp technique, supported by analysis and commentary by Brian "Hash Brown" Calway, one of the most popular and knowledgeable harp players in Dallas, Texas.

I got my harmonica playing style by not copying nothing from nobody. A lot of guys who blow harmonica will listen to another person to get their niche. But I didn't do that. I started out as a trumpet player, and I would use horn lines on the harmonica, transposed. That's how I learned it, because I knew more about other instruments than I did the harp. I don't know about Sonny Boy Williamson, but Little Walter, he did the same thing with the saxophone.

That's why his style was so unique. Sonny Stitt was one of Little Walter's idols. When Walter wasn't working in Chicago, and if he went to where Stitt was blowing, he would always keep some of Sonny's notes in his head and then he would go back home, or maybe go to where a band was playing, and he would remember those notes. He would transpose it from the saxophone to the harmonica. Then the next time he'd have a rehearsal or just be practicing, he would try those same riffs and notes and would work it into his harmonica. That's why his style was so great. If other harmonica players would do the same thing, they could have the style just as good. It may not be no greater, but it could be just as good as his. That's the way I've been, ever since day one. I started out as a trumpet player, but a lot of the notes that I play, it don't sound just like a straight run harmonica. There's a whole lot of harmonica players that think they are playing the blues. But they don't play no classic stuff like "Stardust" or "Misty." That's where my style veers away from a lot of that.

I never did sit down and have somebody teach me how to blow one; I mostly did it on my own. By listening to me play, you would say my style of blowing might sound somewhat like what the next person was doing, but I have different phrases than the average harmonica player. That's how I built up my own style. I never did listen to recordings and try to play along with the patterns, but I would sit down and listen to stuff if it was something that I might want to hear. But I never did try to play like anybody else.

Most harmonica players will blow in and out about the same, but I more or less breathe out, not so much breathe in, through the harmonica. I try to be careful in breathing between notes, because it might get connected to the notes. Breathing out more than in gives me more volume and more bottom end. You won't hear me breathing through the harmonica, because I learned to control my wind. If you use just what wind you need to use, you don't have to breathe so

loud and heavy for your next approach. And a lot of harmonica players, when they take their break, they play too many notes, like they be
playing a guitar solo all over the place. I try to make my breaks support the rest of the song, to be more melodic and not be jamming or
jazzing. I'm about the only one who does it that way. I'm not one of
those lazy players who you see singing or playing the blues. Instead
of expressing themselves or the words they're singing, they're just like
somebody who's reading a *True Detective* magazine or something.

I really don't like playing the harmonica. Everybody expects to
see me doing it, so I want to make my audience happy, but I just don't
enjoy playing it like I used to. I depend on my voice as a singer. If I had
a choice, I would just sing and not play as much harp. It gets me bent
sideways when somebody sees me when I'm out and they say, "Hey,
man, where's your harp?" If you see a carpenter out somewhere, do
you say, "Where's your hammer?" But I don't have to depend on being
a harp player; I'm first a singer. I don't have to fall back on it, like a
guitar player or a piano player has got to do.

Unlike a lot of harp players, I don't like to blow a lot of stuff in the
same key. I like to blow in all the standard keys, if I can, and play the
chromatic, that's the big long one with the button on the end. I can
take a chromatic, and if the guitar player is pretty shifty about what he
or she is doing, I can take that chromatic and make it sound like a big
orchestra. Playing chord riffs, stuff like that. But the harp players who
play in just one or two keys, after a while it sounds like they're playing
the same song. On any night, I might play in about five different keys:
A, C, then G, then that'll put you in a D. I carry seven harps in my
sash, I fill all the pockets up. But usually I play four harps in a night.
They are A, B-flat, C, and G, they're the ones that I blow the most.
Sometimes, if I'm playing a slow blues, I'm going to add the harp
part to it where, a lot of times, there'd be a guitar. I can change keys
without changing harps, depending on what the song is. That's called

blowing cross. I'd be using an A harp, and the next harp would be an E. But if I start in the natural key of A, then I'd be blowing cross into E, like a Jimmy Reed style. I do that by blowing down instead of out. You can do that with a C harp and draw in with the key of G. A B-flat blows out B-flat, and when you suck in, it's F. And then you can go to what is called the third position and you would be in the key of C. It's really strange how it all works.

Hash Brown:

I lived with Sam for two years and took a lot of lessons from him and asked a lot of questions about his playing. He started playing trumpet when he was really young, and I think that helped develop his harmonica playing style in a lot of ways. His phrasing, his note selection, and the fact that he doesn't use a lot of vibrato like a lot of harmonica players do. He'll use what's commonly referred to by harmonica players as a flutter, which is a shaking of the head back and forth to make two notes move. A vibrato is done by a shaking of the hands instead of the head.

There are two different schools of thought on harmonica playing. One way is to play purse-lipped, where you keep your tongue off of the harp to get your sound. The other way is to use your tongue to block the notes. A lot of players from Sam's era either used both methods or did a lot of purse-lipped playing. I believe Sonny Boy Williamson used the first way and Rice Miller used both. Sonny Terry would use more purse-lipped than using his tongue on the harp. Sam always leaves his tongue on the harp when he plays, which makes his approach a little different from those players who split between purse-lipped and using their tongues. Sam mentioned to me once that he likes Sonny Boy a lot more than he likes Little Walter. But he listens to so much music, that I know that from playing with him over the years so many times that he probably knows every Little Walter song inside and out, all the lyrics, and all the harmonica riffs. I've tried to stump him numerous times when he'd come play with us. I'd pull a song out and just start playing it, and he'd know all the lyrics, the arrangement of the song, and where all the harmonica licks were and what they were. He is very well studied because he has a very, very well-developed ear in that area. A lot of people think he tends to get crotchety when he's onstage, as far as what he wants and what he doesn't want. I think that's because it's hard for him to communicate what he does want. He's really adept at playing Chicago and Mississippi shuffle style blues. If someone doesn't know the style, or isn't used to that kind of playing, he may come across as being kind of heavy-handed in trying to tell them what to do. A lot of people misunderstand that as Sam just being a jerk about it. I don't see it that way at all. I see it more as when Sam tries to communicate what he wants, he's more old school about it than some people would like him to be, because they're not practiced in those styles. He's very old school in a lot of ways, as far as hearing something he doesn't like. He would definitely say something about it pretty quick.

His harmonica style to me is classic, late-1940s-to-1950s Chicago-Mississippi harmonica playing. Some of the other players in that style would be Snooky Pryor, Little Walter and Big Walter, Rice Miller, and Billy Boy Arnold. There are quite a few players who play in that style of harmonica language, as I would call it. That's not saying that Sam couldn't write a modern tune, but rather that he's decided to carry on those styles. He'll be modest and say that he doesn't really play that much harmonica, but he really loves it and he does have a unique way of running his phrases. In other words, he doesn't just copy someone else's style on the harmonica. He might hint at some Little Walter or Sonny Boy Number One or Rice Miller, but overall it's a uniquely Sam Myers sound in the way he plays.

He's told me a few times that he got to play quite a bit with Jimmy Rogers. Sam hung out with Jimmy more than Muddy Waters, because Jimmy went out of his way to befriend Sam when he moved to Chicago.

So I think that the harmonica style that Sam developed had something to do with the time he spent playing with Jimmy Rogers. He did play some harmonica when he was with Elmore James, but I think he did more drum work with Elmore than anything else. He told me that during the sessions he did with Elmore for "Poor Little Angel Child" and "Look on Yonder Wall," where Elmore was playing guitar, Sam played harmonica on several songs that were never released.

Sam developed a unique way to get a very, very fat tone by using the air within his hands cupped together. The way he does this is to turn the amp up a little hotter and then not blow as hard through the harmonica, and use his hands to squeeze the air tighter around the harmonica. That gives it a fatter and fuller sound.

Sam's years of playing trumpet probably influenced his harp playing. A lot of harp players also played other wind instruments like the trumpet or saxophone. If you listen to some of Sam's early work, the way he phrases the harmonica is probably imitative of his phrasing on the trumpet. He uses a lot of short, staccato style phrasing, with no vibrato at the end of the notes. He will use vibrato from time to time, but of all the harmonica players I've heard, he's one who does not rely on a lot of vibrato to end his phrases.

A lot of harmonica players nowadays like to play with more of a distorted sound, but Sam comes from the old school where his sound comes through a clean amplifier, even if it's a Fender Bassman amp. He'll push the sound of it a little bit by cupping and squeezing his hands and get a little bit of distortion that way, but the sound that comes out of his amp is almost always very clean, fat and full. Sam will direct the airflow when using tongue-blocking by placing his tongue to the left side of the reed that he's going to blow out of, and the side of his mouth to the right side of the hole. Sometimes he'll put his tongue in the center and suck or blow out of both sides of his mouth to get a chord. But when he's playing single notes, he's blocking all the air off with the side of his mouth on one set of reeds and using his tongue to block the other reeds, and he's blowing through just one, or maybe two, reeds at a time. This gives him a sort of a Louisiana or Mississippi country kind of style, which is a really nice effect.

Sam used to favor Hohner Marine Band harmonicas, but in recent years he's switched to the Hohner Meisterklasse. Right now he's got a full set of those, and when the reed plates go, he gets the Big River harps and takes the reed plates out of those and puts them in the Meisterklasse because they're a little bit cheaper. The Marine Bands don't have the quality that they used to. Plus the wood combs on the Marine Bands would shrink and swell and sometimes cut his mouth, so he switched to the Meisterklasse, which has an alloy comb. He also plays a Super 64 Chromonica for his chromatic work.

CHAPTER 11

THE MUSICIANS' UNION

Organized labor unions for musicians have been in existence for almost a hundred years. Today's American Federation of Musicians seems to be oriented mostly towards providing its members, especially those in symphonic orchestras, with insurance and retirement benefits. But back during World War II, James C. Petrillo ruled the union with an iron fist. Interestingly, his middle name was Caesar, and he was the undisputed emperor of the musicians' union for decades. Petrillo was president of his Chicago local from 1918 until 1940 when he ascended to the national presidency, which he held until 1958. He was so powerful that he was able to single-handedly bring the recording industry to a near standstill during what became known as "Petrillo's War." He became embroiled in a dispute with the few major record companies of the time over royalties that he wanted paid to members for every record pressed. To drive his point home, Petrillo banned all commercial recordings by union members from 1942 to 1944 and again in 1948, when the record companies and the union finally reached a settlement. He may have put a few more dollars in his members' pockets, but an unfortunate casualty of Petrillo's War was the nascent modern jazz era. Few, if any, recordings were made of the earliest developments of the bebop style, although its most important proponents eventually went on to record. But it remains unknown how much of that rich musical heritage was lost.

No doubt a few individuals at the top levels of the union enjoyed prosperity no matter what happened to the music industry, but whether or not the musicians' union was always beneficial to individual members is a matter of opinion.

The musicians' union had some good things that they would do. When you joined the union, you paid your dues, and when you played a union house you got the scale. The house would book bands that had a union contract, and then they automatically would become a union club and would share some of the profits with the union. What they would do, the union had a number of clubs that they would book for you. In the early days of the union, to use the word "musician" you had to be put through a test to become a union musician. There was an audition, and if you could pass that test, automatically you would become a member. Then you paid your dues and you were in. They had a field man that went around with a big book, and if you was sitting in with a band that wasn't union, and it wasn't a union club, they warned you about it. If they caught you playing and your name wasn't on the chart, you'd be the topic of the evening at the union house. If you wasn't a union member, they'd pull you off the stage. Then they'd go talk with the bandleader. The bandleader would have to promise them, if you were going to be working with them, you'd just have to go down to the local and get a permit. It didn't cost much back then for the person to work. Then you'd get union scale, because that's the way the rest of them did it. When you became a unionized musician, they gave you a permit to work until you got your card.

When I took the test, it was over the instruments that I could play. You were supposed to be able to master three. Singing wouldn't necessarily have to be a part of it, but it usually was. But if you were going on as a singer and a musician, you had to be able to play so many different instruments and you had to be able to sing so many different styles. For the test, there would be a whole band there. They'd put a chart in front of you, and then everybody played along with you. You'd be playing different stuff, and then before that song is over you might go through about two or three different instruments. Then you'd do the same way about singing. If you only did blues, they wouldn't call you a musician. Or if you was only a vocalist doing blues, they'd say you was only a blues vocalist. But if you was a musician and a vocalist, you had to do about four or five different styles. So I started out playing trumpet, then I went to do a gospel thing. The guy said, "Well, so much for that," and I said, "Yeah. How far back do you want me to go?" He said, "No, you've gone back far enough."

With James C. Petrillo, a lot of that stuff was going on. He came from New York, and he was the head of the American Federation of Musicians, Local 208. He had another guy in charge if he wasn't there, a Mr. Cooks. He was head of the branch in Chicago. But he was originally from a branch of Local 802 out of New York that used to handle off-Broadway, the Broadway musicals and jazz. They would give you a booklet on what you're supposed to do and what you're not supposed to do. A lot of times it would work, because some guy might come into town and have everything in his band but one certain instrument. If your name was on that bulletin board, then you'd get a gig if you wasn't working. They had such musicians as would stay around the union hall just in case. If a session come up, they would use them on that. A lot of guys made a living doing that, and a lot of them messed their living up by doing it, abusing their privileges, like Elmore James.

He had been in and out of the union so many times, been blackballed so many times. I never will forget, most of the gigs that he did was on his own. If they found out he was playing a club, they'd call the manager and say, "If you book this guy, if he plays your club, you'll never play nobody else." The union was just that strong at the time. But so many people came along who abused their privileges, until now all the union wants is your money. They'll get you a little something to do every now and then but not like they used to. They used to be very strict. But it was the musicians that abused the privileges that they had. It's a very bad thing.

Nowadays, they have insurance for their members. If your instruments got messed up or stolen, they can take care of that for you. But you've got to list your instruments, just like a car, through the union. Like a car can become a total loss, if you're a standing member of the union, you've got the same type of insurance, and they get you new ones. They have health insurance and retirement for you, too, just like a regular job. I don't understand why Texas is a right-to-work state, where you don't have to be in the union to work. Back in the Don Robey days, when I was in and out of Houston, if you wasn't union, you wasn't recognized. Nowadays nobody seems to care if you're union or not.

CHAPTER 12

THE RECORD BUSINESS

Thomas Edison invented the phonograph in 1876 and began selling it in 1887. It wasn't long before the recording industry took off, and the various sharks, con men, and rip-off artists that already plagued the world of live entertainment came right along behind. History does not give us the name of the first recorded musician to be cheated out of what royalties should have accrued to him or her, but the first one started a long chain that continues unbroken to this day. This cheating takes two basic forms. One way is to persuade a musician to sign a disadvantageous contract that would pay some small up-front cash or provide some other gain such as a car, but no royalties thereafter. This was an easy thing for the postwar record companies to do, as many of the older blues artists were limited in their ability to read and understand contracts and were often misled by aggressive recording company officials. The other way would be to promise royalties or even put them into the contract and then simply not pay them. Most musicians who found themselves in this predicament had little or no recourse, because they lacked the money or knowledge of how to fight for their legal rights. The cruelest irony for a musician is to write a song and perform it for a while, lose the rights to that song, and then watch as other artists come along, take the material to record, and reap a handsome payday.

Sam Myers has been mulling over his own experience with this for almost fifty years.

Making a record back in the old days was a lot different than it is now. I liked recording in Chicago or New York better than I did anywhere in the South. For one reason, I never did like it if I had written a song and somebody were to tell me how to sing it, and they can't carry a tune in a bucket. The next thing is, if you got your music set to a song the way you want it to go, you're not supposed to let nobody in the studio change your format around. If you want to add instruments and they're playing the right thing, that's fine. But, man, don't take away anything. I don't like that.

The engineerman was the one calling the shots, or it would be between him and the guy who was handling the record. He would tell you to play it until it sounded right, then you'd go to your next one and you'd do it the same. It may be that something might stand out a little stronger than what you would put into it. That would be good, but don't change the whole thing around unless you know the music. Now, all that was fine, but I do not like a lot of today's sessions, the way people do them. They even got to where, instead of doing stuff raw and clear in the studio, they've gotten into this computer-type thing, computer horns and synthesizers. Now the reason why that is, there used to be a time when you could still find a good engineer. Now, you might want it done this certain way, but the producer has got the money. During the early days, the musicians would tell the producer to get the hell away with his money. But now the producers want something done the way they want it done, and they don't respect the music. Like when Elmore recorded, they never did tell him how to play it. They would say, "Well, what you played, you played too much." Or, "You didn't play it strong enough." Or, "You was a little off the mic when you was singing it." But other than that, he would just run it off. Bam! Do it!

One of the worst things they did back in the early days of recording was to record so much stuff until they had enough material to last them until the musician should happen to die. So if they'd be dead and gone there'd be about three or four more records to come out after that. They would just cut, cut, cut until they'd get something good, and then they'd just put a lot of stuff back on the shelf. You wouldn't hear about it until later, after they're gone. But what they did, they tried to be near right about it as possible, no computer saxophones or stuff like that. No, no. That's where it was so much different back then. Most of the stuff we did, like what Elmore did, you just run it down on one take and then, if that sounded like it was pretty much right, we'd say, "So why don't we hold this one?" Then you do another one, and they'd tell you, "Look, put a little bit more groove into it." Then when you did that, boom! That's it. Two takes and you got it.

The best studios I worked at back then were J&M in New Orleans and Chess in Chicago. What made them special was that the vocalist was separated from the band. You had headphones on, and the vocalist would be closed off from the band in a little booth. Everybody had headphones so you could hear what's going on. That way, you didn't have any bleed-over tracks in that soundproof booth. Everybody could hear one another, and the engineer would just turn up his mic and his headphones to where he could hear himself along with the band. In a case like Elmore's, when he was singing and playing guitar, they had him either of two ways. They could have him out with the band. They had these things they'd put around his head, kind of like baffles, where the other instruments wouldn't bleed into him. Course, they wouldn't be right up under one another, they'd be spread out. But with everybody wearing headphones, they could hear what the next man was doing. And then the other way, Elmore might be in an isolation booth. When I was playing drums over at Chess I had a booth. They couldn't fit nothing in there but me and my drums. They'd close the door and mic everything. Like, "The Sky Is Crying" and stuff like that, they had it mic'd real good. On "Set a Date" and "Can't Hold Out," they had a little echo thing going. It was really nice.

I remember one time in New Orleans, though. Cosimo Matassa, he had just built a new studio. He was one of the best engineers in the south, he taught a lot of people. His studio was at Governor Nicholls and Decatur Street in New Orleans. Before that he had one on Camp Street. They recorded everybody there. He used to be with Sea-Saint, the studio run by Marshall Sehorn and Allen Toussaint, before he got into some trouble with the feds. Cosimo had built a new addition to his studio, and he owed the federal government in back taxes. I'll tell you how he did that. A lot of his sessions he did was what they called "lamplight sessions." That means there wasn't no lights burning in the studio, just like it's closed at night. They just had lamps, so if the union man drove by accidentally, he wouldn't see no lights and he'd go on. It'd be on a night when ain't nothing was supposed to be happening. Not even posted on the union books. Well, somehow they caught that son of a gun, back in 1959. They had a guy to come in who was supposed to be a hell of a musician. But sometimes, if you are really into captivating what's on a person's mind, you can see if something's strange. He came in like everything looked real funny to him. He kept asking, "What's this? What're you doing with this? How do you do this?" Then he would throw it on the guys like, "I can play the music to a lot of songs, but all these different instruments, what are they for?" Actually he was a federal guy. He worked for the FBI, and he came in posing as a musician to get the low-down on the lamplight sessions.

That's how Elmore did a lot of his sessions, but this particular session wasn't Elmore. It was some guys out of Jackson, Mississippi, who they were recording, and they was also recording Lee Dorsey. He got a big hit record out of that session called "Get Out of My Life, Woman." That was a big one for him. He also recorded "Ya Ya," the one that goes, "Sittin' on my la la, waitin' on my Ya Ya." That was a cut from a lamplight session. He also did some records for Bobby Robinson on Fury.

So, what the FBI guy did, he just wandered around the studio, saying things like, "Oh, I like that part," and he called Cosimo "Cos," just like he had been knowing him all the time. He didn't say the kind of things a musician would, like, "Hey, would you play that back for me? Let me hear what I did, so I know how to balance the rest of it out." I was pretty skeptical about stuff like that. Now here comes this guy, new in town, don't know anybody, actin' stupid like there wasn't nothing going on, he didn't know nothing, but how did he happen to know Cos by name? Nobody had introduced nobody to nobody; we all just came in and started recording.

So, he was talking with Cos and he said, "Well, Cos, that sounded good," and we kept on until we got that part right. And then he said, "Well, it's a done deal," you know, like everything was over with. He said, "Yep, everything is done, it looks like it's going to be done for a long time." And then everybody laughed, like, "What the heck is this guy talking about?" He had this little thing in a horn case. He reached in and hit a button and all of a sudden, these guys start knocking on the door. Cos said, "Well, heck, don't nobody know that we're here, but I'm still going to go see who it is," and he walked to the door to open it and tell them they wasn't open for business. When he opened the door, the guys just pushed it wide and came on in. And this FBI musician said, "Yep, just like I said, looks like it's going to be a long time before there's going to be another one." Then everybody was surprised. I thought there was something funny going on, but I didn't ever speak right out; that'd be a dead giveaway. So I was right in what I thought, because he gave us all a break. He said, "Well, you guys are not the ones that we want." He named 'em off: Marshall Sehorn, Bobby Robinson, and Cosimo Matassa. Cos was the main one, that's who they wanted. The FBI man asked us all to leave. Well, naturally, we didn't want to go to jail, so we just got the heck out of there.

Back in the old days at Chess, Willie Dixon ran the show in the recording studio. It wouldn't take them a long time to get it together to rehearse and record. Most of the times, what Willie would do, he would play it along with them. Then, if they wanted to do it a different way, as long as they used the song, they'd run in and do that. Before the day is gone, they'd record it. When all this would be happening, the guys, instead of recording just enough to do an LP, they would be in the studio recording different takes on different songs to see how many they could record. A session to them was something like fifty to a hundred songs. That would be a twelve-, fourteen-, sixteen-hour stretch of work, sometimes more than that. We'd go in around two in the afternoon, and we'd record all night. From the time we'd go in, getting the arrangements and recording it, getting a good balance on the tape, we'd record enough songs that would last us until maybe six or seven o'clock in the morning. If the guys wanted coffee, somebody would leave out at midnight and go pick up some coffee and bring it back to the studio. They'd take a break just long enough to eat a snack and have some coffee. A lot of them, the reasons their records sound so wavy, they would always be having a drink during the session. They may say, "We're going to do this with such and such a musician," and then sometimes they'd just do so many with whoever's in the studio to record with them. There were better recordings then, because you didn't have a session like an open door thing. A lot of times nowadays, anybody can come in off the street, enter in your session, and interrupt you. "If I was you, I'd play it like this, or I would do this, I would do that." Back then the only way you would be able to get into the studio is if you were affiliated with the session. People just couldn't come and go as they pleased. That's what messes up a lot of records nowadays. You know, they think you're having a party, and everybody gets to have their input. But somehow they get it done.

When Elmore James was recording, he would just run one song down with the band, and on the second one, that would be the first take of it. After about three takes, it's a done deal. He would just pick something at random, come up with a beat, and everybody would just blend in. Most of his stuff he did that way was slide; it sounds somewhat the same anyway. He would use different notes, but his early material was basically the same unless he recorded something with a horn section. I have a lot of friends in this modern technology deal, but I like to take my hat off to the guys from the old school who're gone and some who're still around. To me, that's just common courtesy. They were the pioneers that showed the way; it had never been done before them. You should always give respect to your peers.

In 1964, there was a gentleman named Willie Roy Sanders who recorded an early version of a song called "Crosscut Saw." He was a construction worker; he and Albert King had worked together doing road construction on some jobs in the upper western part of Arkansas, and from there back down to West Memphis, building highways and clearing land for other stuff to be built. When Willie Roy's record came out, "Crosscut Saw" was the number one blues song at radio station WDIA in Memphis. The people who Willie Roy had a contract with, somehow they decided to go with Albert King instead, and later on he recorded that same song. He stepped it up a little bit, and that's the way he made it his own. Now everybody knows it as Albert King's song, and he didn't even write it. Willie Roy didn't get no money from doing his own version, either.

There's one thing I can say, even back from day one, and that's people always want to point the finger at the white musician for stealing the black man's music. But the thing with Albert King and Willie Roy Sanders, that was black on black, against black. That's not the only thing that has happened. Black musicians have been doing that stuff since day one, taking and ripping one another off. They all look at it like, "The white man did this, the white man did that." It has always been a rip-off thing with either race of musicians. It's sad, but it's true.

It used to be that you could just change some words in the song, and then you say it was your own. If you want to have a hit record out there with somebody else's song, the right thing to do is to contact the sole owner who has the copyright to that song and get their permission. But now, with the public domain thing, a person can record anything that you've recorded. It could be your song, but after thirty years they would not have to give you a dime or even get your permission to do it. The law says you can do that, but to me it's a wrong thing. The music business has had its ups and downs and its rights and its wrongs ever since day one. It's just something that you have to deal with. But if there was a way that you could get money for it, it would be a good thing. Like with "Sleeping in the Ground," there's a whole lot of people today who know that I wrote it, but they'll tell me, "Man, you don't own nothing." But if it's my own words, my lyrics and my own composition, then why don't I own it? The law says after thirty years it's public domain, but that didn't do me no good before the thirty years was up.

There are many others who haven't gotten what's rightfully due to them on their music. Other people would have to record their material before it would be recognized that they were the ones who did it. I'm one that falls right into that category. Personally speaking, I don't want just anything. I want specifically one thing, and that's what's rightfully mine.

I said all that just to say one thing: as long as there is music, there's gonna be a way that somebody is going to try to connive and downgrade you in what you're doing. If I had thought about doing back then what I have in mind to do now, "Sleeping in the Ground" would never have appeared on records done by a whole lot of people that are doing great for themselves, but I'm not getting a dime.

There are a lot of musicians who have released that song, and the only thing I ever got from it was a name as the writer of that song. It's all right to have a name, but where could you spend that at? I asked Johnny Vincent about it once, and he said that different people had recorded it, and as soon as he got some royalties on it, I would, too. The next thing I know he had sold his company, then the next thing after that, he died.

Robert Cray and Eric Clapton and several other people whose names I do not know have recorded "Sleeping in the Ground." That particular song is on at least ten other records. It was on Eric Clapton's deal twice; he had a box set with it that went platinum. But not a dime for me, though. So what can you say about that? People ask me to do the song, and I say, "I don't mean to be rude in no way, but as soon as I get some money for doing this song, I'll be *too* glad to sing it for you." Some people understand, but some people look at it like me being smart.

If anybody wants to know the meaning behind "Sleeping in the Ground," the song explains itself, simply because anybody who does any writing of any song usually does nothing but tell a story that faces the facts of life. A song has a pattern, just like anything else. A song could be a story, or a story can be divided up into a song. It's about everyday things, as facts about life itself. "I'd rather see you / Sleeping in the ground / Than to be around here / Knowing you're going to put me down." That explains itself. The purpose of the whole thing is, you're telling the story of a loved one who was there only for what was in it for them. You gave them all the money you had and everything that you owned. Being conscious of it, meaning that one day, even though you know it would be the wrong thing to happen, you'd like to see that person sleeping in the ground. You might wonder yourself, why would you even want to be around, when you know she's about to put you down? You know it's happening because as soon as you get broke during this relationship, it's better to be away from that person.

A lot of songs that I've written myself and recorded for other people, I've gotten royalties from, but not "Sleeping in the Ground." I recorded it again on Black Top for Hammond and the late Nauman Scott. I thought I was treated fairly by them because my contract was up when I recorded it on one of the Anson Funderburgh and the Rockets records. I think they treated me fairly about that, for me not to be a recording artist for them. It was just being on somebody else's record, but it was my song.

We're going to go way back a number of years to what happened with the late John Lee Hooker, who was originally from Clarksdale, Mississippi. He left home at an early time, back in the forties, went to Chicago and hung around awhile and then went to Detroit. He played the original clubs there like Henry's Swing Club and various bars around the area and all over the south and west sides of Detroit. Henry's Swing Club was on Hastings Street before they cut the expressway across it. That used to be the street in Detroit for the blues. John Lee Hooker used to play there and he wrote this song, "Boogie Chillen." During that time, he recorded other songs that he wrote, like "Sally Mae," "Devil's Stomp," "Nightmare Blues," and a Big Joe Williams tune, "Baby Please Don't Go." He did these recordings under an assumed name, "Texas Slim." He may have been under some kind of commitment or contract that he wasn't able to draw any royalties under his name, so he recorded under that name in order to get paid. But people, they knew it was John Lee Hooker when they heard his record. A lot of times the name protects the innocent, but if you're innocent, what kind of name would you have to use other than your own, to protect yourself? He died a few years ago, just when he had begun to draw royalties from back-written songs that he did. John Lee and Clarence "Gatemouth" Brown are two people from that industry who, along with myself, have come up against this sort of thing. They were the ones I know personally who didn't get a lot of the money due them.

Don Robey kept Clarence "Gatemouth" Brown off the rolls for right at almost twenty years. He was working for Don and recording a lot of material that was his own. This was at Duke Records out of Houston, Texas. A lot of the people that recorded for that label wound up just making records and a big name for themselves, but no money. A lot of guys back then thought on the same level, to cheat you out of what little you had. They would say, "Hey, man, you got a big record here, you need to hit the road, they're waitin' for you." They had an old saying that was a bad thing, and I never did like for nobody to call me that. "You got a big record out there. Go get 'em, tiger!" Go get what? You're not getting any money, what is out there for you to go get? The money's there, but are you getting it?

For a lot of the Elmore James sessions I was on, I didn't get more than the session pay, and that was all I was supposed to have gotten. Course I never did write any of Elmore James's songs, and I don't expect nothing from that. I was just a member of his band. But stuff that's rightfully mine, I figure if it's a song that I wrote, then I deserve to get my money for that.

Like all those Jimmy Reed records, over there at Vee-Jay Records. Jimmy was forty-eight when he died; his wife, Mary, was living on welfare, and she didn't get a dime for his music. I feel like people should have that equalization of what they got going, what is rightfully theirs. But you got shysters everywhere, man. Take Freddie King. Look at what a Dallas wimp did to him. After Freddie King died, some kind of way he got his hands on the plates and the rights of Freddie

King's material. By Freddie King being a Texas guy, this guy went to his wife and got all of Freddie's songs that hadn't been released and dumped it off on Black Top Records. They made a little money off it, too. But at a time when it could have been done better and made some better money, Black Top went out of business. It was just a downhill situation.

CHAPTER 13

STORIES FROM THE ROAD

Any musician who has traveled the world and played with the wide range of artists that Sam Myers has is bound to have a treasure trove of humorous anecdotes. Anson Funderburgh, Sam's bandleader, collaborator, and friend for some twenty years, also contributes a trio of road stories. The stories that follow are not quite as colorful as some that the author has heard, but they have the virtue of being printable.

When I was with King Mose and the Royal Rockers back in 1957, we had a real good group; we were real friendly with each other. Unlike a lot of musicians, we were playing just as many or even more of the white business establishments than the other bands. We played at different fraternities at Ole Miss in Oxford, Mississippi, and at Mississippi State in Starkville. I never will forget one fraternity party that we played. It was for the gentlemen of Pi Kappa Alpha and their sorority. This man walked up with a half-gallon of corn whiskey, but he did not want me to have a drink. He told King Mose, "All you guys can have some except for Sam, because he rolled his eyes at me." So Mose told the guy, "No, that's just the way the guy's eyes is. He's partially blind." The guy said, "Oh, I'm sorry about that." Now Mose had a fifth of Early Times which me and him were drinking on. He said to the guy,

"Me and Sam will have a drink out of my bottle, just for you saying that." I said, "I have to have some water or something like a soft drink to chase it with." The only thing they had to drink was RC Cola. Mose said, "I drinks mine straight," and I said, "That's why you can wind up being drunker than me." He laughed, but I wound up at the end of the night drunker than he was. Anytime when you drink liquor with a soda, it's the sweetness along with the fumes of the liquor that makes you drunk, so it's better to drink it with water. We laughed about it after that.

There was a song that I had listened to Bobby "Blue" Bland do, one of his all-time hits called "Turn on Your Love Light." The same particular night, Mose had just gotten out of the hospital for a hemorrhoid operation, and he was getting ready for us to take a break so he could go use the washroom. I was really bent sideways with him, because they all were drinking amongst themselves, and I had to drink with this guy after him saying that I rolled my eyes at him. So right at the end of the part where I was supposed to sing, "I get so lonely in the middle of the night / I need you darling, everything will be all right / Turn on your love light and let it shine on me," instead I sang, "Turn it up, turn it up!" and I just kept on singing. Mose was trying to give me the signal to end the song because he had to go to the washroom. I kind of hated that I did that afterwards, but I really did put him through something.

Then by it being during the winter months, we had to ride in a '46 Roadmaster Buick with our instruments and all of us piled up in the car. He did use the washroom, but it was on himself and we had to ride all the way from Starkville to our next gig in Greenville, Mississippi, to play at the Elks Lodge, with him not going to the washroom like he should've went. He said, "Man, the next time somebody tell you to stop a song, you will." I said, "Hey, man, we had a groove going; I couldn't just stop." He said, "Well, you'll know the next time." He wasn't a man who would take whatever you do against your pay; he would always figure out something else. But I would always be staying one step ahead of him.

I had some spyglasses made by a good friend of mine that worked in a welding shop. He took the glass part out of each one of the eyes of this pair of binoculars, and they would hold about a pint of liquor apiece. I had him to melt some lead to pour into it and seal the eye part up. We played at Forest City, Arkansas, between Little Rock and Memphis, in the summer, at the Forest City Country Club. That was about one of the saddest gigs that I ever remember playing, because we asked for water and nobody had any water or sodas for us, just for the audience. I said, "Man, we should got us some bottled water or something, 'cause this is going to be a hard gig to play." We played a whole four-hour gig without a drop of anything to drink but me. I didn't have a soda or nothing to chase the liquor that I had with me in those spyglasses, so I was higher and feeling better than any of them there. They said, "Man, you got something going on, you on some kind of drugs?" I said, "No, only Jack Daniel's." They was really bent sideways with me about doing that!

We went on after that to Memphis to play the King Cotton Festival. Instead of it being a big outdoor festival, it was in different clubs in different parts of the city. We all went to set up our instruments at the club, and everybody was hungry. My lady friend at the time, who was my son Willie Earl's mother, had fixed me up with a big bag of chicken sandwiches. I told the boys, "Every man for himself," just teasing 'em. I had three dollars and twenty cents, and when we stopped at this liquor store on Beale Street right off of Third, I went on in to get me a pint of Ballantine scotch. Matter of fact, Elmore was with us then, with King Mose. He had left Chicago to go with us. This was about in the summer of '57, and everybody was broke. If they had enough change, maybe they could chip in together and maybe got one meal for one person and split it up. But I had the three dollars and some few cents on my own, so I went and got my liquor and I took a big drink. Elmore says to me, "Man, you know, we all here, I got a little cash, and we all hungry. You don't believe in sharing, do you?" I said, "Sure. But if you got some money, you can get you something to eat and you could have a drink with me. Why don't you just buy some food and then we'll all eat. But otherwise I drinks by myself." I kept my liquor to myself, but I shared out that big bag of sandwiches with the boys.

Around Chicago, when I wasn't working anywhere or if I had an off night, I would always get out to see some of the cats I never did hang with over on the West Side, unless I was doing my gig with Elmore James at Silvio's. I'd go and see a lot of the guys, but mainly the Howlin' Wolf. Strange as it may seem, if you're a man that's thirty or forty years old, as long as you're not being obnoxious or anything of the sort, you're supposed to be able to do what you want to, within reason. But over the years, a lot of people never did know of this happening, but the Wolf would whip the members of his group like they were kids. They were not allowed to have a drink unless he approved it. He would always tell the guys when they'd take a break, "All right now, watch yourself!" He'd be sittin' there having a scotch or rum with his friends, and he'd be telling his band, "All right, look out there, the Wolf got his eye on you!" He would take them back into the dressing room and whup them like they was little kids. Not many people may have heard that over the years, but it was true. By him being as tight as he was, he ran a tight group, and then he kept a good band better than most of the guys did. If they were onstage and one of them messed up a song or something, the same thing happened. Wolf said to me one night, "I've seen you play with a lot of guys, but you've never come up on my bandstand." I said, "Wolf, I tell you what, I don't know you that well, but for me and you to be good friends it would be best for me not to do that, because of the way I am. If you made a mistake and forgot that I wasn't a member of your band, I don't care how big you are, they don't have no work in the penitentiary for a blind man. 'Cause, man, I'd kill you!" He just said, "Heh, heh, heh, we gonna always be friends." I said, "Yeah, no other way to do but be friends. 'Cause the day that happen to me, they'll either have a double funeral, or yours." He just laughed some more and went on.

Elmore used to have a saying, "You run your mouth, but I run my business." There was a lady that Robert Lockwood, Jr., used to run with. He just up and gave her to Elmore after he decided he didn't want her no more. Lockwood was working at Silvio's as the house bandleader. Different musicians would come by on different nights to play in a jam. They held them a lot different back then than the way they do now. Like you see across Texas, they do a lot of open mic stuff, but back then these jams would be professional people displaying what they know, doing it together. If you played on a guy's bandstand at a real jam session, your instrument had to be tuned and you played what you knew. It wasn't no guesswork. So one night, we were all sitting around like musicians do, people like Lockwood, Odie Payne, Fred Below, myself, and just a bunch of guys shooting the breeze. Everything that Elmore played, if he didn't play in the key of E, when he wasn't using a slide he used a capo. We used to call it a clamp. He got up to make a telephone call, and when he came back, Lockwood had stole his capo and hid it from him. Elmore said, "Man, I got the perfect song but I've got to have my clamp. Damn, where is it?" All the other guys hollered, "I don't know! I haven't seen it!" He said, "Well, whoever it was that took my clamp was having sex with his mama." That's when Lockwood spoke and said, "Hey, you didn't ask me about your damn clamp. But I'll tell you this much: I'm the one that got it and I'm not gonna give it back to you. And you must have had sex with your mama, but I didn't have none with mine. But I'll do one more thing for you that nobody else has done. I gave you a woman the other day, and now I'm gonna show you how to play without that damn clamp. Then, when you face the world, you'll know how to play something." And after Lockwood showed Elmore the technique of how to play without a capo, he never used one again.

I never will forget one other time, at the Chess Records studio, Robert Lockwood, Jr., and Luther Tucker was getting ready to do a Little Walter session. The song was "Temperature." It goes, "My baby gives me a high temperature." People who know Lockwood know that he was a creator and innovator of a lot of those sessions. He said to Luther, "Man, this might be something here." But Luther said, "Yeah, man, but instead of me playing that, how about faking it?" So Lockwood looked at him hard and said, "Hey, man, we're not faking nothing here! Today we're playing!" So Luther finally got into his head how Robert wanted the music to go, and he played it. That was one of Walter's biggest sellers.

When I first started with Anson, the guys in the band were real musical-orientated. They would always see what songs we could do, and they would always be inquisitive about different ways we could do them, to make them better for our performances. The new guys in Anson's band are a little different now than in the old days, but they're real cool guys. One of the funniest things that happened, it was one of Anson's songs that we used to do a lot. I didn't tell him, but there was a lady sitting there in the audience who said, "I'll give you a nice tip for this song." I tried to sense him into what was happening. It was a simple song, and the lady, after she told me this, she gave me a twenty-dollar bill. But Anson hollered to her, "Sorry, we don't do that song anymore." So after he had told her that, well, there wasn't nothing else I could say but ask her, "Would there be anything else you'd like to hear?" She said, "You're sounding good, just play anything." I asked her name, and I called it out and then played the next song. And that made that twenty-dollar bill rightfully mine!

We were riding one day through Chicago, going out to Spellman. That's out by one of the universities there. Doug Swancey was driving the bus. Now he drums with Kenny Traylor's band out of Fort Worth. We was riding through the city up to where they had pulled down the ramp to the Dan Ryan Expressway. There was untied steel and everything sticking out, and I said to Doug, "What you have to do is take the outer lane of the Dan Ryan. You don't want to go up onto where the guys are working." He said, "I know, but I can't get over." I said, "Just take the outer lanes where the other cars are going and it will get you right to where you need to be." He said, "I can't do that," so I said, "Why in the hell can't you do it?" He said, "Well, for one thing, I can see where I'm going." I said, "I got two things against you. I used to live here, and I know my way around Chicago pretty good. You can see and I can't, but I sure know what the hell I'm doing and what way to go." And it broke his heart when he ended up having to go the same way I told him to go.

Another time we were coming out of Cleveland heading into Detroit. We were going to a club called Sully's where we were going to be playing. We were on the expressway north of Toledo on Highway 75, so there was a lot of traffic. But before all this happened, we had stopped to have some work done on the bus. I had eased on over to the mechanic and he said, "I can't understand why this motor's not running free, but I'll fix what they say." I said, "What you need to do is to take that governor all the way off so the bus will run freely." He said, "I hadn't thought about that. I'll just take it off, and he won't know it until he tries to drive slow when he's not supposed to." I was sorry afterwards that I told the guy to take it off, because we was going through Toledo getting ready to hit the outer lanes of 75 going up north to Detroit. We was about fifty miles out and the traffic was pretty heavy. We was on a bridge and Doug swung around and said, "Boy, we're moving now!" and I said, "Yeah, you're moving pretty good." Then he swerved back in, and just as he went to get back over in his lane, this car was coming pretty fast, and by the bus being as long as it was, it hit this guy's car and almost turned it over. So Doug got right in the middle of the bridge and stopped, but the traffic couldn't get by him. He just froze. I said, "You hit that man's car! You better get your long-haired ass out and go back and see about that man, see is anybody hurt." He kept saying, "I ain't going, I ain't going, I ain't going." So Anson came up to the front and got out and went back there. I said, "If I was that man and I wasn't hurt, I'd get me a sledgehammer and come up here and beat you until you really turned green because you messed up his car." He just kept saying, "I ain't going, I ain't going," just like that. So finally we went on and made the gig. It wasn't too long before he left the group and started working with somebody else, but everybody, they're all still friends. So that was a pair of Doug Swancey extravaganzas.

Mike Judge was another guy that was in the band. [*Author's note: Mike Judge is the creator of the TV shows* Beavis and Butthead *and* King of the Hill, *as well as the movie* Office Space. *His animated character Beavis is drawn with a blond pompadour that resembles Anson's.*] He was a bass player, and I thought there was something up with his talent as far as him being in the band. He was a beautiful musician, a great bass player, but he was always coming up with these different sounds. Like somebody would say something to him, and he'd make a sound like a siren, like the cops was after him, or he'd remember what somebody had told him and he would be imitating them. That's how his career took off, and he's been going ever since. I think a lot of guys envy him, but if you got talent and can display it in a way where it could be beneficial to you, hey, you should glory in your spunk, you know.

The funniest thing that ever happened to me anywhere, whether it was on the road or not, was before I was declared as a diabetic. I used to not only make whiskey, I drank a lot of it, too. Back when I was working with Elmore in Jackson in a club called the S&S, Camel cigarettes were only thirty-five cents a pack. That's all I've ever smoked. I was going to the telephone, and I had it in mind to get me a pack of cigarettes and then use a dime to get the operator to call my mother. So what I did, I went over to the telephone and I put thirty-five cents in it. Then I grabbed the telephone's little knob and was pulling and jerking on it. The club owner, John Simpson, came over and said, "Hey, man, what in the hell are you doing?" I said, "I'm trying to get some cigarettes out of this S.O.B." He said, "Man, you can't get no cigarettes out of this thing. Wait a minute." He hit the change release thing and my money came back, and a little more. He said, "I'm going to split this with you since we got lucky. But I'm going to take thirty-five cents and go over and get you a pack of cigarettes." That was about as drunk as I've ever been.

Another time, I had been drinking all day. Then I went to work at night at that same club, the S&S. We were getting ready to hit the road after that, to go up to Cleveland to play a club there called Gleason's Bar, at Fifty-fifth and Euclid. The guy had a hotel and a bar where we played. I had been drinking all that day, then I was going to go home where I was living at 127 West Davis Street, and we would leave out at eight o'clock the next morning. All the guys, by having to hurry home to get their gear and stuff together and maybe take a nap or two, they all went off and left me. I could have got a cab to go home, but I was still hanging around in the bar. I had drank me a whole lot of liquor that night, but I never did get too wasted when it come to doing my show earlier in the evening. But by this time, I was off drinking with different guys.

There was this guy standing at the bar who I did not recognize as being a deputy sheriff. John Simpson and his uncle, Percy Simpson, was standing there talking to the guy. I said, "Well, it's about time for me to get on in." I was just sober enough to know that. The guy said,

"Well, you've about had a night," and I said, "Yeah, I've about had one but I got to head on and hit the road." He said, "If you're not going to get a cab or have nobody take you, I'll drop you off." I said, "Hey, man, that's all right, let me know when you get ready." He said, "I'm ready when you get ready." I said, "I'm gonna have one more." I had drunk right then about a half of a half-pint of whiskey, sitting there at the bar. I never did look up to see who the guy was. We goes out, he caught me by the arm, and we walks out and I gets in the front seat with him and he goes around to the driver's side. I remember this, oh, I remember this as if it happened just a few minutes ago. I thought something was strange that we got downtown mighty fast, so just as he turned onto Davis Street, I went to ask him what kind of work did he do. About that time I heard his radio go off and say, "All available cars, there's been a gasoline truck in a wreck out on Highway 80 West." I raised up and I said, "Holy shit!" and he looked at me and laughed and said, "What's the matter? I thought you knew who I was!" I was riding with the man who could have took me anywhere but home. We were almost right in front of my house when the radio had come on. I hopped out, and I was sober and steady as a judge! And ever since then, whenever he would see me, it didn't matter if it was in broad daylight, he would ask me, "Did you ever get sober? Did you ever get straight?" and we'd just laugh. That was in 1959, and he was a white cop. But he was a blues lover and he had been coming by that club to pick up a shakedown, one of those kinds of deals.

I did have one kind of scary thing to happen to me. In Cincinnati, Ohio, we were doing a festival there. This woman climbed up on stage and started hitting me with her handbag. She didn't say nothing before, she just walked up and whaled the devil out of me. The woman said I had jilted her out of a house and left her with a retarded child. I said, "Oh, no, not me!" I was just took by surprise. The cops, they were supposed to have security there onstage. Now why did they let something like that happen? And I took it that she was on drugs, you know. Everybody had a big laugh about it, but I said, "I'm going to tell you all something. If I had known that was going to happen, they would probably be picking up pieces of her out in the audience." And then I got pissed off at the cops because they didn't want to hear nothing that I said about it. I could have went over their heads and got restitution in another way, but I didn't. I don't care who's in the audience or who I'm playing with, I've always been careful since then. I don't care where I am, I always have a protective thing with me whenever I'm onstage. Sad but true. I usually carry a knife or a gun or something. And where I'd be a dummy, I'd say, see here, I got this, I got that. If you're gonna do something, or if you got something to do something with, if the other person has got it in mind to do harm to you, you're not supposed to let him know that you're ready for him.

Anson Funderburgh:

Back somewhere in the eighties, we'd go down to Austin and do these benefits for Clifford Antone, whose club was always in dire straits. This was back when the place was on Guadalupe Street in South Austin. They had all the usual Austin people there, plus the Kentucky Headhunters. It was just me and Sam who went, and we sat in with the house band. I think it was George Raines on drums and Kim Wilson on harp and singing; that's all I can remember. I think there's still a tape of it somewhere. Now, some of these nights at Antone's could go on forever. They'd shut the doors and play 'til six in the morning if they wanted to. The Kentucky Headhunters were the headliners that night, and they closed the regular show. Later on, after the audience and most of the employees were gone, they started in jamming, and Sam wanted to get up with them. When there's music to be played, he's always ready to be a part of it. He might say, "Oh, no, I don't want to," and kind of play it down for a minute, but if nobody asks him, he'll be the first one to start trying to sneak up onto the stage.

*Anyway, he was up there playing, with Clifford Antone on bass,
Derek O'Brien on guitar, Kim was on harp, and Sam was singing. There
was a guy who played guitar for the Kentucky Headhunters who at this
time was playing piano. I think his name is Richard Young. This guy had
real long hair, was kind of heavyset and wore glasses. Sam kind of half-
way introduced the people that were up there, and when he got to the guy
who was playing piano, he said, "You know, I'm not sure what the young
lady's name is who's playing piano . . . ," and everybody just died laughing. Derek went up to him and told him it was a guy who was playing
piano, and Sam just said, "Oops! Slippers! Sorry about that!" and just
went on like nothing had happened.*

*Another time we were playing at the Grand Emporium before I was
married to my wife, Renée, even before she started traveling with us as a
singer. She was at the show selling CDs for us. She and Sam were really
good friends. He'd buy her little presents, and she'd take him to go buy
suits, that kind of thing. They had gone out to do something earlier that
day, so he wanted to get her up on the stage that night and introduce
her. He said, "Now, I'd like to get one of the most angelic specimens of
femininigy up here . . . ," and before he could say Renée's name, some
other woman who he had been talking to at the bar ran up onto the
stage and hugged him and kissed his cheek. Sam couldn't figure out what
to do. Here he had this other girl up here whose name he didn't know.
He looked over at me, and I didn't know who she was. He finally bent
down and said, "What's your name, honey?" You could hear him over
the microphone when he was asking her what her name was. When she
finally got down, he looked over at me and said, and you could still hear
him through the microphone, "What the hell was she running up here
for? I was trying to introduce Renée!" The whole place could hear him!*

*Once Renée started traveling with us, we had this dog that would
come along. Her name was Muddy. We were playing this outdoor show
down by the river outside of Kansas City. It was on a flatbed truck, and*

Mud was up there with us. She was the greatest dog in the world, went everywhere with us. Even Sam loved that dog. He was always accusing us of not feeding her, and he would always be giving her some of his food, fried chicken or whatever he had. He'd always give her a little bite. So we were playing that show, and nobody had a hold of Muddy. She was down at the truck when Sam started singing, "I'd rather drink muddy water . . ." I guess Muddy must have thought he was calling her. She came down out of that truck, ran up onto the stage and started playing around, chasing Sam's feet. Sam was startled, jumped back and started doing this little dance while Muddy was running around his ankles. It looked like they were dancing and the audience just went crazy, thinking this was all part of the act.

CHAPTER 14

SAM'S BEST FRIEND, ANSON FUNDERBURGH

Anson Funderburgh, of Plano, Texas, has been a stalwart of Texas blues guitar for almost thirty years. At the age of fifteen he started playing at local parties and in clubs like the notorious Cellar in Dallas with his first band, Sound Cloud. A year after he graduated from high school in 1973, Anson headed for the blues mecca of Austin to join a newly formed house band called Blue Norther. But the group never jelled, so Anson did a few gigs with Doyle Bramhall and Marc Benno and for a while was a member of the Nightcrawlers. That band had earlier been a springboard for Anson's hometown friend, Stevie Ray Vaughan. After a year Anson headed back home to Dallas. He and the late Brent MacMillan put together a short-lived band called Delta Road. Anson's next band, Bees Knees, was a so-called "tropical rock" band. After two albums in three years, Anson left Bees Knees and returned to his blues roots, reuniting with Doyle Bramhall for a stint in Doyle's Dallas version of the Nightcrawlers. Anson and Doyle opened for national acts Albert King and Lightnin' Hopkins at the old Granada Theater in Dallas. Five years after leaving high school, Anson struck out alone and the first version of the Rockets was born.

I started the Rockets in 1978. Darrell Nulisch was the first singer in the band. We used to work around the Dallas area, then we started branching off. We played in Louisiana, Mississippi, Arkansas, and Oklahoma, kind of spiraling out. In 1982 we played a little place called the George Street Grocery in Jackson, Mississippi. This was right about when our first record came out, "Talk to You by Hand." A guy came in and asked me if I wanted to meet Sam Myers. I said, "Yeah, I'd love to meet Sam Myers." At that time, Darrell and I were doing "My Love Is Here to Stay," which is a song of Sam's that he released in 1957. So he brought Sam up and introduced him to us. Sam sat in, and it was just great. We thought it was the coolest thing. We played at that place quite a bit. It was Freddie Walden, Doug Rynack, and Jackie Newhouse when we first started playing there and later Eddie Stout, and Darrell and me. Every time we'd go over there, we'd all go get Sam and just hang out.

There used to be a place called the White House where we liked to go eat lunch or dinner. It seemed like all of Sam's friends and all of his relationships kind of originated around a dinner table. We all became such good friends, every time we'd visit Jackson we'd pick up Sam and go out to eat, go to the record store, go look for antique clothes, go to the pawnshops, just do whatever, goofing off. Back in those days, we'd play for three or four days. We'd usually play George Street on Thursday, Friday, and Saturday and then their booking agent, Malcolm White, would have an outdoor event or something for us on Sunday, some sort of little afternoon deal. So we were there at least once every three months, and we just all really became great friends with Sam. I had a record deal with Black Top, so instead of making another Rockets record, I got into Hammond Scott's ear about him coming out to see Sam again and maybe doing a record with him. Hammond drove up to Jackson from New Orleans and hung out with us and visited with Sam again. Hammond knew of Sam from before, so we talked it over and decided to do it. In '84 Sam and I made that record, "My Love Is Here to Stay." Sam wasn't in the band at that time. It was just a little side project to do something different and to get his name back out there again. I think it's probably one of our best records, I really do. It's a good, strong record. In '84, Sam would have been almost fifty years old, and he just sounded great on it, the whole band did.

So we just kind of tooled along. We'd fly Sam out and include him in some of our performances and tours. He played the San Francisco Blues Festival and the Battle of the Harmonicas out there with us. We played in New Orleans, just a little added deal to the show, and to promote the record for Hammond. And then in '86, when Darrell left the band, hell, I just called Sam up and asked him if he wanted to start to work with us, to move to Dallas and start playing. It just seemed like the thing to do. He wasn't doing much at the time, and we could use the record that we made to promote ourselves as a calling card and get some work. He said yeah, so I borrowed Fingers Taylor's van and one of his old Bassman amps and one of his JT30C harmonica microphones. We borrowed all that stuff from Fingers and moved Sam to Dallas, and that's how we started with Anson and the Rockets featuring Sam Myers. That was in April 1986. He and I rehearsed for about a month, and we started to work in May.

Within six months I took Fingers's van back and bought our own van and fixed it up. Sam and I hit the road really hard. Hell, we worked 260 to 280 days a year for the first five or six years. I booked the band up until about the first part of 1990, when we hired the David Hickey agency. They really helped us to get out there even further. It's been a neat trip. You kind of look up and you think, wow, it's been almost twenty years that's slipped by.

One of my favorite Sammy stories is from when we were recording "My Love Is Here to Stay." I didn't know much about Sam personally at that time. I mean, I did and I didn't, because we had hung out together some, but you really don't know someone until you're with them all the time. The first night after he joined us we took him out to eat. He ordered *a large combination pizza and a large plate of spaghetti. I thought to myself when he ordered all that food, man, he'll never be able to eat all that. I'll be dadgummed, he made a liar out of me. When we left, there wasn't a noodle left of the spaghetti or a crumb left of the pizza. It just really knocked me out.*

After we made that record, we used to fly Sam out to gigs when we'd stay gone for two or three weeks. He'd play the festival gigs that could afford to pay for something like that. On one of our first trips out to California, we picked Sam up in L.A. We were going to do several shows in L.A., work our way up the coast, and end up the weekend playing the San Francisco Blues Festival. So we picked him up and got all his stuff from the luggage area and loaded it into the van. Sam got in and he said, "My old feet hurt. Look in that little old brown briefcase there and hand me my easy-steppers." Everybody thought, OK, what's that, a comfortable pair of shoes? It was actually a harmonica case and when we opened it up, here on top of all these harmonicas was this stinking, filthy pair of house shoes that he had sitting on those damn harmonicas that he'd been putting in his mouth and blowing on. All of us just got the biggest kick out of that. We said, "This here's a serious road man!"

I think the thing that's held us together for so long is that Sam and I have a pretty good respect for one another, and I think we really do love one another. Our friendship and our love for the music has been the vehicle for Sam to play the music he really loves, to play blues and get out there and gain fans. Even though sometimes it hasn't been absolutely perfect, like maybe the band didn't jell exactly like we wanted it to with certain members or whatever, but all in all it's been about a love for the music and our friendship. Even when we're not on the best of terms, we'll call each other all the time to see what's going on. Personally, I really love him; he's just like part of my family. I've known Sam since 1982, so I've known him for twenty-four years now and he and I have actually worked together for almost twenty years.

When we first started playing as Anson Funderburgh and the Rockets featuring Sam Myers, there weren't a whole lot of guys doing what we were doing with someone who was as authentic as Sam and someone that was like myself. I consider myself a traditionalist, even though some people might say I was more contemporary because I'm a younger white guy that's been playing this kind of music. Sam and I have really been fortunate; when we came out and first started doing the thing, man, the press, they loved us. There's no telling how big a stack of stories and articles I have about this band. It's pretty amazing how much people just embraced us. Music is a funny thing; there are so many talented people out there that never make it, who you never hear of. It's hard to know what really makes things work. Even though our success on a bigger picture is pretty small, for the blues picture our success has been very large. The last twenty years I can say haven't always been easy, but it's been pretty damn good, man, and it's been fun. The first ten years of it were real fun. Over time, people's priorities change, but Sam and I have had a pretty damn good run of it. We've been a whole lot luckier than a lot of people.

Sam as an artist is very unique, because to me he wasn't a guy that sounded like Little Walter or that really big, heavy, heavy harmonica of Big Walter. He has his own little twist to things, kind of a country taste or flavor to it. He plays it with such different dynamics. I'm not sure I know exactly how to explain what he does or how he does it, but since he's been playing with this band he's kind of taken that country sound and electrified it. On a lot of his earlier recordings he'd just play straight harmonica into a bubble mic. In the later years with us he'd use a microphone, and it's a little bit bigger of a sound, but it's still not exactly the same kind of bigness as Little Walter. His sound is different; he's got his own phrasing with the harmonica. I find him very unique in that he's found a cross between the country sound and more of an electric sound. Kind of like Muddy did, when he was playing with a bottleneck by himself or with a really small band, and then there's the later Muddy with the electric guitar and a full-blown band. It's kind of the same kind of sound, but electrified; it sounds different. Sam has done the same kind of thing with his style. He's still playing the same way as his early stuff, but he's electrified it, and it's very unique to me. I think he's his own guy.

In writing songs with Sam, he and I seem to have a process that we go through to blend our ideas together. Maybe I'll have some sort of lick that I'm playing. Or it might be some progression that I've been working on, and I'll start playing it for him. Maybe I'll have some ideas for the theme of the song or some lyrics to try out. I might say that I want a song that's in the key of E, with kind of a Lightnin' Hopkins or Jimmy Rogers kind of style. Then I'd start playing things and maybe get an idea about having been on the road for a while and call out some of the cities that we've been to, or maybe the roads and highways we've been on. Just crazy stuff like that, and we'll talk about it some. Then Sam might come in with a set of lyrics that he's been working on. I'll always set up a little boom box recorder, and I'll start playing some of the licks and figures behind it. I'll whisper the words to Sam and he'll sing them, or maybe it's something that he's worked on and he'll sing it and I'll try to play some part for it. We just kind of go from there. Sometimes it doesn't make any sense, so once we've recorded it on the boom box and we listen back to it, maybe we'll say the first verse we sang might work better as the third verse, or vice versa. So we do things like that, swap it around some and get some rough ideas of where we want the song to go. Maybe John Street will come over and play piano while we're going through this process. I've got a small recording studio in my house, so sometimes we'll just build the song there, with a keyboard for John and my guitar and Sam. We can put drums down from the piano, and while it's not perfect, it gives us a pretty good idea of where we want to go when we get in the studio. When you're spending a few hundred dollars an hour for studio time, you really want to have things a little bit more together than just going in and winging it. That can be very expensive these days. But we've actually had a lot of fun writing songs for our records. We try to make at least half of it original and half of it traditional-sounding songs that we like to play.

I think you can measure success as a musician in several different ways. There's the guy can play a little bit of everything. I respect people who can play anything or sing anything; they just have the ability to play music. But it moves me more, and this is just a personal thing, to see someone who has their own style, like B.B. King. I can hear him play three notes and I know it's B.B. King. I can hear Sam play three notes on the harmonica or sing a little, and I know it's him. He has a unique style that's all his own. As musicians, that's what we all strive for, to have some unique quality about us that makes us different and sets us apart from everyone else.

DISCOGRAPHY

LABEL	CATALOG NO.	TITLE	RELEASED
45 RPM SINGLES			
Ace	536	My Love Is Here to Stay Sleeping in the Ground	1957
White Label (Dutch label, probably same personnel on Ace sessions)	1955	Rhythm with Me	1957
Fury	1035	You Don't Have to Go Sad, Sad Lonesome Day	1960
Ace	3027	You're So Fine The Things I Used to Do, Sam Myers, hca	1979
Mid South	NR 15681	Back in My Baby's Arms (B side); billed as Sam "Blues Man" Myles [sic]	1984
RECORD ALBUMS			
WITH VARIOUS MUSICIANS:			
TJ	1030	*Down Home in Mississippi*	1979
TJ	1040	*Mississippi Delta Blues*	1980

TJ	1002	*Mississippi Delta Blues Band: In Europe*	1981
TJ	1050	*Mississippi Delta Blues Band*	1981
TJ	1054	*Mississippi Delta Blues Band, Chromatic Style*	1986
TJ	1056	*San Francisco Blues Band*	1986
TJ	1060	*Mississippi Delta Blues Band: Greatest Hits*	1986

WITH ANSON FUNDERBURGH AND THE ROCKETS:

Black Top	1032	*My Love Is Here to Stay*	1986
Black Top	1038	*Sins*	1987
Black Top	1049	*Rack 'Em Up*	1989
Black Top	1068	*Tell Me What I Want to Hear*	1991
Black Top	1077	*Through the Years: A Retrospective*	1992
Black Top	1111	*Live at the Grand Emporium*	1995
Black Top	1140	*That's What They Want*	1997
Rounder	619573	*Change in My Pocket*	1999
Rounder	619619	*Which Way Is Texas?*	2003

AS SAM MYERS:

Electro-Fi	3383	*Coming from the Old School*	2004

APPEARS WITH THE FOLLOWING ARTISTS:

Black Top	1046	Snooks Eaglin, *Out of Nowhere* "Young Girl," Sam Myers, hca	1988
Black Top	1050	Joe "Guitar" Hughes, "If You Want to See These Blues," Sam Myers, hca	1989
Cannonball	29108	Hash Brown, *Hash Brown's Texas Blues Revue* "My Daily Wish," "Dog in a Man (Ways of a Man)," Sam Myers, vcl; "Got You Where You Want Me," "Sad and Lonesome," Sam Myers, vcl/hca; "Ain't Gonna Let You In," vcl w/ Zuzu Bollin	1999
Socan	401	Robin Banks, *Honestly* "Don't You Love Me Like That," "I Need a Lovin' Man," "None A' Nothin'," "My Kinda Lover," "Thunder and Lightnin'," Sam Myers, hca	2001
Topcat	4022	Jim Suhler, *Dirt Road* "Shake Hands with the Blues," Sam Myers, hca	2002
P-Vine	3775	Snooks Eaglin, *Out of Nowhere* Sam Myers, hca	2003
Blue Bella	1003	Nick Moss, *Count Your Blessings* "Hey Hey," "She Brought Life Back to the Dead," Sam Myers, vcl/hca	2003

APPEARS ON THE FOLLOWING ELMORE JAMES RERELEASES:

Relic	7040	*Dust My Broom: The Best of Elmore James, Vol. 2*	1992

Rhino	71190	*The Sky Is Crying:* *The History of Elmore James*	1993
Charly	BM28	*Standing at the Crossroads*	1993
Collectables	8829	*The Complete Fire and* *Enjoy Sessions*	1995
P-Vine	112522	*Best Blues Masters, Vol. 2*	1998
Rhino	79803	*Blues Masters:* *The Very Best of Elmore James*	2000
Buddha	99781	*Shake Your Money Maker:* *The Best of the Fire Sessions*	2000
P-Vine	2889/9	*The Sky Is Crying:* *The Legendary Fire/Enjoy Sessions*	2003

APPEARS ON THE FOLLOWING COMPILATIONS:

Sundown Reissue	CG 709-01	*Blow by Blow: An Anthology* *of Harmonica Blues* "My Love Is Here to Stay"/ "Sleeping in the Ground"	1979
Vivid Sound Reissue	VS-1011	*The Kings Sing the Blues:* *Vol. 2* "My Love Is Here to Stay"/ "Sleeping in the Ground"	1979
P-Vine Reissue	6101/6102	*N.Y on Fire:* *Bobby's Harlem Rock, Vol. 2* "Poor Little Angel Child," "Little Girl" (with Elmore James), "You Don't Have To Go," "Sad, Sad Lonesome Day"	1986
Black Top Reissue	1044	*Black Top Blues-A-Rama* "Pawnbroker," That's Alright,"	1988

		"Suggestion Blues," "Changing Neighborhoods" (with Anson Funderburgh)	
Charly Reissue	1208	*New York Blues, Vol. 2* "Poor Little Angel Child," "Little Girl" (with Elmore James)	1989
Savage Kick Reissue	508	*Savage Kick Vol. 8: Black Rock 'n' Roll* "You Don't Have to Go"	1990
Black Top Reissue	2	*Black Top Blues-A-Rama— A Budget Sampler* "20 Miles" (with Anson Funderburgh)	1990
K-Tel Reissue	846	*Blues: The New Breed* "Chill Out" (with Anson Funderburgh)	1991
Black Top Reissue	1066	*Blues Cocktail Party* "Bombastic," "Look What You're Doing to Me," "Make a Little Love" (with Anson Funderburgh)	1991
Black Top Reissue	1073	*Black Top Blues-A-Rama, Vol. 6: Live at Tipitina's* "20 Miles," "Hold That Train, Conductor," "Look on Yonder Wall," "One Room Country Shack," "Feel So Bad," "Can't Stop Lovin' My Baby" (with Anson Funderburgh)	1992
Black Top Reissue	1078	*Soul Survey: A Blues Sampler* "Tell Me What I Want to Hear" (with Anson Funderburgh)	1992

Black Top Reissue	1079	*Blues Harmonica Spotlight* "My Love Is Here to Stay," "Since We've Been Together" (with Anson Funderburgh)	1992
Black Top Reissue	1083	*Blues Guitar Spotlight* "Dog in a Man (Ways of a Man)" (with Anson Funderburgh)	1992
Rhino Reissue	71123	*Blues Masters, Vol. 3:* *Texas Blues* "Changing Neighborhoods" (with Anson Funderburgh)	1992
Ace Reissue	2028	*Genuine Mississippi Blues* "Sad and Lonesome," "You're So Fine," "Money Is My Downfall," "Gold Tail Bird"	1993
Capricorn Reissue	42009-2	*The Fire/Fury Records Story* "You Don't Have to Go"	1993
Rollin' & Tumblin' Reissue	RT 2607	*Heavy Harp* "My Daily Wish," "Sam's Jam"	1994
Charly Reissue	3	*Modern Blues Anthology:* *Ain't Times Hard* "You Don't Have to Go"	1995
Rhino Reissue	72017	*Blues Masters, Vols. 1–5* "Changing Neighborhoods" (with Anson Funderburgh)	1995
Black Top	1122	*Blues, Mistletoe &* *Santa's Little Helper* "Sam's Christmas Blues," "Lonesome Christmas," "Young Girls Drive Me Wild (at Christmas)" (with Anson Funderburgh)	1995

Black Top Reissue	1124	*Black Top Blues Vocal Dynamite!* "Tomorrow Will Find Me the Same Way" (with Anson Funderburgh)	1995
Celebration of Blues Reissue	2519	*A Celebration of Blues:* *Great Guitarists, Vol. 3* "Down At J. J's" (with Anson Funderburgh)	1996
Celebration of Blues Reissue	2521	*A Celebration of Blues:* *Great Slide Guitar* "Make a Little Love Tonight" (with Anson Funderburgh)	1997
Celebration of Blues Reissue	2523	*A Celebration of Blues:* *Great Swing Blues* "Mean Streak" (with Anson Funderburgh)	1997
Easydisc Reissue	7038	*Texas Blues Party* "20 Miles" (with Anson Funderburgh)	1997
Easydisc Reissue	7048	*Blues Harp Power* "Rack 'Em Up" (with Anson Funderburgh)	1997
Platinum/A&M Reissue	161286	*Essential Texas Blues* "Changing Neighborhoods" (with Anson Funderburgh)	1997
Official Reissue	52544	*Papa Lightfoot and Sammy* *Myers: Blues Harmonica* *Wizards* "Sleeping in the Ground," "My Love Is Here to Stay," "You Don't Have to Go," "Sad, Sad Lonesome Day," "Look on Yonder	1997

Wall" (with Elmore James),
"Poor Little Angel Child"
(with Elmore James)

WestSide Reissue	570	*Tuff Enough, Vol.3: The Ace Blues Masters* "Sleeping in the Ground," "My Love Is Here to Stay"	1998
WestSide Reissue	812	*Mark Lamarr's Ace Is Wild* "My Love Is Here to Stay" (alt. take)	1998
Platinum/A&M Reissue	161407	*Jingle Blues* "Sam's Christmas Blues" (with Anson Funderburgh)	1998
Charly Reissue	220	*Blues Harp Bosses* "You Don't Have to Go"	1998
Easydisc Reissue	367072	*Blues Guitar Masters* "Mean Streak" (with Anson Funderburgh)	1998
Easydisc Reissue	367073	*Blues Harp Hotshots* "Bombastic" (with Snooks Eaglin)	1998
Ace Reissue	710	*Harp Blues—The Greats!* "Sleeping in the Ground"	1998
WestSide Reissue	579	*Genuine Mississippi Blues . . . Plus* "Gold Tail Bird" (take one), "Money Is My Downfall," "You're So Fine," "Sad and Lonesome," "Take Me Where You Go," "Gold Tail Bird" (take two)	1999
Richmond Reissue	3008	*We Got the Blues for You* "Sleeping in the Ground"	2000

Varese Reissue	61131	*Harp and Soul* "What's Wrong, What's Wrong" (with Anson Funderburgh)	2001
Music Blitz Reissue	30011	*Handy Award Nominees, Vol. 1* "Change in My Pocket" (with Anson Funderburgh)	2001
Past Perfect Reissue	325	*Rhythm & Blues Goes Rock & Roll, Vol. 2* "You Don't Have to Go"	2002
WestSide Reissue	240	*Shuckin' Stuff—Rare Blues from Ace Records* "Got My Nose Open," "19 Years Old" (Johnny Littlejohn with Sammy Myers, hca), "My Love Is Here to Stay" (alt.), "Sleeping in the Ground" (alt.), "My Love Is Here to Stay" (demo), "Sleeping in the Ground" (demo)	2002
Rounder Reissue	612171	*Box of the Blues* "Change in My Pocket" (with Anson Funderburgh)	2003
Fuel 2000 Reissue	61273	*Blues, Booze, Harps and Guitar* "What's Wrong, What's Wrong" (with Anson Funderburgh)	2003

SONG CATALOG

Sam's most famous song, "Sleeping in the Ground," was recorded in December 1956 at Trumpet Studios in Jackson, Mississippi, on Johnny Vincent's Ace label. Some of the artists who have covered this song:

Robert Cray, *Who's Been Talkin'* (Tomato 7041, 1980)
Eric Clapton w/Blind Faith, *Crossroads* (Polydor 835261, 1988)
Omar and the Howlers, *Blues Bag* (Bullseye CD-BB-9519, 1992)
Steve Winwood, *The Finer Things* (Polygram 516860, 1995)
Duster Bennett, *I Choose to Sing the Blues* (Indigo 2091, 1998)
Duster Bennett, *Bright Lights, Big City* (Castle 81292, 2003)
Honeyboy Hickling, *Straight from the Harp* (Music Maker 943, 2000)
Blind Faith, *Blind Faith 2000 Deluxe Edition* (Polydor 549529, 2001)
Greg "Fingers" Taylor, *Hi Fi Baby* (Warehouse Creek 114, 2003)

Songs written or co-written by Sam Myers:

After Hours When the Joint Is Closed – Myers
The Amateur (She's Gone) – Myers, A. Funderburgh
Bombastic – Myers, A. Funderburgh, Ford Eaglin
Burning Fire – Myers
Change in My Pocket – Myers, Renée Funderburgh
Changing Neighborhoods – Myers, A. Funderburgh
Chill Out – Myers, A. Funderburgh
Coming from the Old School – Myers
Country Boy – Myers
Dew Is Falling – Myers
Don't Quit the One You Love for Me – Myers, A. Funderburgh
Gold Tail Bird – Myers

Hep Cats in Big Town – Myers
Highway Man – Myers, A. Funderburgh, R. Funderburgh, Pat Whitefield
I Done Quit Getting Sloppy Drunk – Myers
I Got a Thing for the Voodoo Woman – Myers
I Got the Blues – Myers
I'm Innocent – Myers, A. Funderburgh, Danny Cochran, Jim Milan
I've Been Dogged by Women – Myers, A. Funderburgh
I Want a Wife – Myers, A. Funderburgh, Hammond Scott
I'm Tired of Your Jive – Myers
Lemonade – Myers, A. Funderburgh
Let You Slowly Bring Me Down – Myers
Missing Person – Myers, A. Funderburgh, Cochran, Milan
Money Is My Downfall – Myers
My Heart Cries Out for You – Myers
My Love Is Here to Stay – Myers
Packing Up My Blues – Myers
Poor Little Angel Child – Myers, A. Funderburgh
Rack 'Em Up – Myers, A. Funderburgh
Sad, Sad Lonesome Day – Myers
Sam's Christmas Blues – Myers
Shedding Tears of Laughter – Myers
Since We've Been Together – Myers, A. Funderburgh
Sleeping in the Ground – Myers
Suggestion Blues – Myers, A. Funderburgh
Tell Me What I Want to Hear – Myers, A. Funderburgh, Matt McCabe, Milan, Scott, Harvey Shield
Things Have Changed – Myers
Tomorrow Will Find Me the Same Way – Myers, A. Funderburgh
Trying to Make You Mine – Myers, A. Funderburgh
Turning My Life Around – Myers, A. Funderburgh
20 Miles – Myers, A. Funderburgh
Waiting on You, Mamma – Myers
What's Wrong, What's Wrong – Myers
Willie Jo – Myers, A. Funderburgh, R. Funderburgh
You Don't Know What Love Is All About – Myers
Young Girls Drive Me Wild – Myers, A. Funderburgh

SAM MYERS, ELMORE JAMES, AND BOBBY ROBINSON SESSIONS

ELMORE JAMES SESSIONS:

Chief/Vee-Jay Records, Chicago 1957. Elmore James (guitar), Wayne Bennett (second guitar), J. T. Brown (tenor sax), Jimmy Lee Brown (bass), Johnny Jones (piano), Earl Hooker (second guitar), Sam Myers (drums).
1. The Twelve-Year-Old Boy
2. Coming Home
3. It Hurts Me Too
4. Knocking on Your Door
5. Elmore's Contribution to Jazz

Fire Records, Chicago (Chess Studios), 1959. Elmore James (guitar), J. T. Brown (tenor sax), Homesick James (bass), Johnny Jones (piano), Sam Myers (drums), Eddie Shaw (alto sax).
1. Bobby's Rock
2. The Sky Is Crying
3. Held My Baby Last Night
4. Make My Dreams Come True

Chess Records, Chicago, 1960. Elmore James (guitar), J. T. Brown (tenor sax), Homesick James (bass), Johnny Jones (piano), Sam Myers (drums).
1. The Sun Is Shining
2. Stormy Monday
3. Madison Blues
4. Can't Hold Out
5. Whose Muddy Shoes

Fire Records, New York, 1960. Elmore James (guitar), Johnny Acey (piano), J. T. Brown (tenor sax), Sam Myers (drums), Riff Ruffin (second guitar), unknown (second saxophone).

    1. Rollin' and Tumblin'
    2. I'm Worried
    3. Done Somebody Wrong
    4. Fine Little Mama
    5. Can't Stop Loving You
    6. Early One Morning
    7. Strange Angels
    8. She Done Moved
    9. Something Inside of Me
    10. Harlem Angels

Fire/Fury Records, J&M Studios, New Orleans, 1961. Elmore James (guitar), Sammy Lee Bully (bass), Sam Myers (drums, harmonica), Mose Taylor (drums), Moose Walker (piano).

    1. Look on Yonder Wall (Myers, harmonica, Mose, drums)
    2. Shake Your Moneymaker (Myers, vocals)
    3. Sunnyland (Myers, drums)
    4. Poor Little Angel Child (Myers, vocals)
    5. Little Girl (Myers, vocals)
    6. Go Back Home Again (Myers, harmonica)

Fire Records, Beltone Studios, New York, 1960. Elmore James (guitar), Johnny Acey (piano), J. T. Brown (tenor sax), Sam Myers (drums), Riff Ruffin (second guitar), Paul Williams (bass), unknown (second saxophone).

    1. Baby Please Set a Date
    2. I Need You

Fire Records, Beltone Studios, New York, 1961. Elmore James (guitar), Johnny Acey (piano), J. T. Brown (tenor sax), Danny Moore (trumpet), Sam Myers (drums), Riff Ruffin (second guitar), Paul Williams (bass).

    1. Anna Lee
    2. Standing at the Crossroads

Enjoy Records, A-1 Studios, New York, 1963. Elmore James (guitar), Moose Walker (piano), Sam Myers (drums), Paul Williams (bass).

    1. Dust My Broom

BOBBY ROBINSON SESSIONS:

Fury Records, J&M Studios, New Orleans, 1960. Dave Campbell (piano), Sam Myers (vocals and harmonica), Mose Taylor (drums).
1. Sad, Sad Lonesome Day
2. You Don't Have to Go
3. Sad and Lonesome

APPEARANCES, AWARDS, AND HONORS

MOTION PICTURES

China Moon (1994). In this thriller starring Ed Harris and Madeline Stowe, Sam and Anson with the Rockets make a cameo appearance as a bar blues band and perform "Tell Me What I Want to Hear."

AWARDS AND HONORS

W. C. Handy Awards, with Anson Funderburgh and the Rockets:
2004 – Traditional Album of the Year, *Which Way Is Texas?* (Rounder/Bullseye)
2000 – Song of the Year, "Change in My Pocket"
1994 – Band of the Year
1992 – Band of the Year
1989 – Sam Myers, Vocalist of the Year
1988 – Band of the Year
    Song of the Year, "Changing Neighborhoods"
    Album of the Year, *Sins* (Black Top)
    Sam Myers, Instrumentalist of the Year, Other (Harmonica)

January 6, 2000 – Inducted into the Farish Street Walk of Fame at the Alamo Theater, Jackson, Mississippi. Shared honors with Dorothy Moore and the late Sonny Boy Williamson II (Rice Miller).

February 17, 2006 – Received Governor's Award for Excellence in the Arts and named Blues Ambassador by the Mississippi Arts Commission, presented by Haley Barbour, Governor of Mississippi.

BIBLIOGRAPHY

Calway, Brian. "Interview with Sam Myers." *Blues and Rhythm* 137 (March 1999): 26–27.

Erlewine, Michael, Vladimir Bogdanov, Chris Woodstra, Cub Koda, and Stephen Thomas Erlewine, eds. *All Music Guide to the Blues*. 3rd. ed. San Francisco: Backbeat Books, 2003.

Franz, Steve. *The Amazing Secret History of Elmore James*. Marceline, Mo.: Wadsworth Publishing Company, 2002.

Harrison, Alferdteen. *Piney Woods School: An Oral History*. Jackson, Miss.: University Press of Mississippi, 1982.

Howse, Pat, and Jimmy Phillips. "Godfather of the Delta Blues—H. C. Speir. An Interview with Gayle Dean Wardlow." *The Peavy Monitor* (1995): 34–44.

Jones, Laurence Clifton. *The Spirit of Piney Woods*. Old Tappan, N. J.: Fleming H. Revell Company, 1931.

Leadbitter, Mike, and Neil Slaven. *Blues Records 1943 to 1970: A Selective Discography, Vol. 1 (A to K)*. London, UK: Record Information Services, 1987.

Leadbitter, Mike, Leslie Fancourt, and Paul Pelletier. *Blues Records 1943 to 1970, Vol. 2 (L to Z)*. London, UK: Record Information Services, 1994.

Leiter, Robert David. *The Musicians and Petrillo*. New York: Octagon Books, 1974.

Murray, Charles Shaar. *Boogie Man: The Adventures of John Lee Hooker in the American Twentieth Century*. New York: St. Martin's Press, 2000.

O'Neal, Jim, and Amy O'Neal. "Sam Myers in Jackson." *Living Blues* 3 (Autumn 1970): 19, 21.

O'Neal, Jim, and Peter Lee. "Sam Myers: Blowing It Off the Top." *Living Blues* 85 (March/April 198): 10–21.

Romulo, Beth Day. *The Little Professor of Piney Woods: The Story of Professor Laurence Jones*. New York: J. Messner, 1955.

Rowe, Mike. *Chicago Blues: The City and the Music*. New York: Da Capo Press, 1975.

Ryan, Marc. *Trumpet Records: An Illustrated History with Discography*. Winter Haven, Fla.: Big Nickel Publications, 1992.

————. *Diamonds on Farish Street.* Jackson, Miss.: University Press of Mississippi, 2004.

Wilson, Christine, ed. *All Shook Up: Mississippi Roots of American Popular Music.* Jackson, Miss.: Mississippi Department of Archives and History, 1995.

INDEX